How To Win

Friends

&

Influence People

How To Win Friends & Influence People

DALE CARNEGIE

WILLWIN PUBLICATION

How To Win Friends & Influence People

by *DALE CARNEGIE*

Edition **2026**

Published by
Willwin Publication
E-mail: **Willwinpublication@gmail.com**

Printed and bound in India

EIGHT THINGS THIS BOOK WILL HELP YOU ACHIEVE

1. Get out of a mental rut, think new thoughts, acquire new visions, discover new ambitions.

2. Make friends quickly and easily.

3. Increase your popularity.

4. Win people to your way of thinking.

5. Increase your influence, your prestige, your ability to get things done.

6. Handle complaints, avoid arguments, keep your human contacts smooth and pleasant.

7. Become a better speaker, a more entertaining conversationalist.

8. Arouse enthusiasm among your associates.

This book has done all these things for more than ten million readers in thirty-six languages.

This Book Is Dedicated to a Man Who Doesn't Need to Read It: My Cherished Friend

HOMER CROY

CONTENTS

✱ INTRODUCTION ✱

Dale Carnegie (1888–1955) was an American writer, lecturer, and pioneer in the field of self-improvement and corporate training, best known for his timeless work, ***How to Win Friends and Influence People*** (1936).

Born into poverty on a farm in Missouri, Carnegie started his career as a salesman before pursuing his passion for public speaking. He began teaching public speaking classes at the YMCA in New York, where he quickly realized his students needed help not just with speaking, but with all aspects of human relations, self-confidence, and communication.

His lectures and subsequent books synthesized these practical principles for success, focusing on empathy, genuine interest in others, and motivation. *How to Win Friends and Influence People* became a massive international bestseller, offering advice on how to handle people, make them like you, win them to your way of thinking, and change them without giving offense.

Carnegie also established the **Dale Carnegie Course** in 1912, which grew into a global training institute. His later notable works include ***How to Stop Worrying and Start Living*** (1948). His legacy lies in demystifying social skills and self-development, making his time-tested principles a cornerstone of the modern self-help and professional development industry.

↣ Preface To Revised Edition ↢

How to Win Friends and Influence People was first published in 1937 in an edition of only five thousand copies. Neither Dale Carnegie nor the publishers, Simon and Schuster, anticipated more than this modest sale. To their amazement, the book became an overnight sensation, and edition after edition rolled off the presses to keep up with the increasing public demand. **How to Win Friends and Influence People** took its place in publishing history as one of the all-time international bestsellers. It touched a nerve and filled a human need that was more than a faddish phenomenon of post-Depression days, as evidenced by its continued and uninterrupted sales into the eighties, almost half a century later.

Dale Carnegie used to say that it was easier to make a million dollars than to put a phrase into the English language. **How to Win Friends and Influence People** became such a phrase, quoted, paraphrased, parodied, used in innumerable contexts from political cartoons to novels. The book itself was translated into almost every known written language. Each generation has discovered it anew and has found it relevant.

Which brings us to the logical question: Why revise a book that has proven and continues to prove its vigorous and universal appeal? Why tamper with success?

To answer that, we must realize that Dale Carnegie himself was a tireless reviser of his own work during his lifetime. **How to Win Friends and Influence People** was written to be used as a textbook for his courses in Effective Speaking and Human Relations and is still used in those courses today. Until his death in 1955 he constantly improved and revised the course itself to make it applicable to the evolving needs of an ever-growing public. No one was more sensitive to the changing currents of present-day life than Dale Carnegie. He constantly improved and refined his methods of teaching; he updated his book on Effective Speaking several times. Had he lived longer, he himself would have revised **How to Win Friends and Influence People** to better reflect the changes that have taken place in the world since the thirties.

Many of the names of prominent people in the book, well known at the time of first publication, are no longer recognized by many of today's readers. Certain examples and phrases seem as quaint and dated in our social climate as those in a Victorian novel. The important message and overall impact of the book is weakened to that extent.

Our purpose, therefore, in this revision is to clarify and strengthen the book for a modern reader without tampering with the content. We have not "changed" **How to Win Friends and Influence People** except to make a few excisions and add a few more contemporary examples. The brash, breezy Carnegie style is intact—even the thirties slang is still there. Dale Carnegie wrote as he spoke, in an intensely exuberant, colloquial, conversational manner.

So his voice still speaks as forcefully as ever, in the book and in his work. Thousands of people all over the world are being trained in Carnegie courses in increasing numbers each year. And other thousands are reading and studying **How to Win Friends and Influence People** and being inspired to use its principles to better their lives. To all of them, we offer this revision in the spirit of the honing and polishing of a finely made tool.

– Dorothy Carnegie (Mrs. Dale Carnegie)

✧ How This Book Was Written—And Why ✧

During the first thirty-five years of the twentieth century, the publishing houses of America printed more than a fifth of a million different books. Most of them were deadly dull, and many were financial failures. "Many," did I say? The president of one of the largest publishing houses in the world confessed to me that his company, after seventy-five years of publishing experience, still lost money on seven out of every eight books it published.

Why, then, did I have the temerity to write another book? And, after I had written it, why should you bother to read it?

Fair questions, both; and I'll try to answer them.

I have, since 1912, been conducting educational courses for business and professional men and women in New York. At first, I conducted courses in public speaking only—courses designed to train adults, by actual experience, to think on their feet and express their ideas with more clarity, more effectiveness, and more poise, both in business interviews and before groups.

But gradually, as the seasons passed, I realized that as sorely as these adults needed training in effective speaking, they needed still more training in the fine art of getting along with people in everyday business and social contacts.

I also gradually realized that I was sorely in need of such training myself. As I look back across the years, I am appalled at my own frequent lack of finesse and understanding. How I wish a book such as this had been placed in my hands twenty years ago! What a priceless boon it would have been.

Dealing with people is probably the biggest problem you face, especially if you are in business. Yes, and that is also true if you are a housewife, architect, or engineer. Research done a few years ago under the auspices of the Carnegie Foundation for the Advancement of Teaching uncovered a most important and significant fact—a fact later confirmed by additional studies made at the Carnegie Institute of Technology. These investigations revealed that even in such technical lines as engineering, about 15 percent of one's financial success is due to one's technical knowledge and about 85 percent is due to skill in human engineering, to personality, and the ability to lead people.

For many years, I conducted courses each season at the Engineers' Club of Philadelphia, and also courses for the New York Chapter of the American Institute of Electrical Engineers. A total of probably more than fifteen hundred engineers have passed through my classes. They came to me because they had finally realized, after years of observation and experience, that the highest-paid personnel in engineering are frequently not those who know the most about engineering. One can, for example, hire mere technical ability in engineering, accountancy, architecture, or any other profession at nominal salaries. But the person who has technical knowledge plus the ability to express ideas, to assume leadership, and to arouse enthusiasm among people—that person is headed for higher earning power.

In the heyday of his activity, John D. Rockefeller said that "the ability to deal with people is as purchasable a commodity as sugar or coffee." "And I will pay more for that ability," said John D., "than for any other under the sun."

Wouldn't you suppose that every college in the land would conduct courses to develop the highest-priced ability under the sun? But if there is just one practical, common-sense course of that kind given for adults in even one college in the land, it has escaped my attention up to the present writing.

The University of Chicago and the United Y.M.C.A. Schools conducted a survey to determine what adults want to study.

That survey cost $25,000 and took two years. The last part of the survey was made in Meriden, Connecticut. It had been chosen as a typical American town. Every adult in Meriden was interviewed and requested to answer 156 questions—questions such as "What is your business or profession? Your education? How do you spend your spare time? What is your income? Your hobbies? Your ambitions? Your problems? What subjects are you most interested in studying?" And so on. That survey revealed that health is the prime interest of adults and that their second interest is people; how to understand and get along with people; how to make people like you; and how to win others to your way of thinking.

So the committee conducting this survey resolved to conduct such a course for adults in Meriden. They searched diligently for a practical textbook on the subject and found not one. Finally, they approached one of the world's outstanding authorities on adult education and asked him if he knew of any book that met the needs of this group. "No," he replied, "I know what those adults want. But the book they need has never been written."

I knew from experience that this statement was true, for I myself had been searching for years to discover a practical, working handbook on human relations.

Since no such book existed, I have tried to write one for use in my own courses. And here it is. I hope you like it.

In preparation for this book, I read everything that I could find on the subject—everything from newspaper columns, magazine articles, records of the family courts, the writings of the old philosophers, and the new psychologists. In addition, I hired a trained researcher to spend one and a half years in various libraries reading everything I had missed, plowing through erudite tomes on psychology, poring over hundreds of magazine articles, searching through countless biographies, trying to ascertain how the great leaders of all ages had dealt with people. We read their biographies; we read the life stories of all great leaders from Julius Caesar to Thomas Edison. I recall that we read over one hundred biographies of Theodore Roosevelt alone. We were determined to spare no time, no expense, to discover every practical idea that anyone had ever used throughout the ages for winning friends and influencing people.

I personally interviewed scores of successful people, some of them world-famous inventors like Marconi and Edison; political leaders like Franklin D. Roosevelt and James Farley; business leaders like Owen D. Young; movie stars like Clark Gable and Mary Pickford; and explorers like Martin Johnson, and tried to discover the techniques they used in human relations.

From all this material, I prepared a short talk. I called it "How to Win Friends and Influence People." I say "short." It was short in the beginning, but it soon expanded to a lecture that consumed one hour and thirty minutes. For years, I gave this talk each season to the adults in the Carnegie Institute courses in New York.

I gave the talk and urged the listeners to go out and test it in their business and social contacts, and then come back to class and speak about their experiences and the results they had achieved. What an interesting assignment! These men and women, hungry for self-improvement, were fascinated by the idea of working in a new kind of laboratory—the first and only laboratory of human relationships for adults that had ever existed.

This book wasn't written in the usual sense of the word. It grew as a child grows. It grew and developed out of that laboratory, out of the experiences of thousands of adults.

Years ago, we started with a set of rules printed on a card no larger than a postcard. The next season we printed a larger card, then a leaflet, then a series of booklets, each one expanding in size and scope. After fifteen years of experiment and research came this book.

The rules we have set down here are not mere theories or guesswork. They work like magic. Incredible as it sounds, I have seen the application of these principles literally revolutionize the lives of many people.

To illustrate: A man with 314 employees joined one of these courses. For years, he had driven and criticized and condemned his employees without stint or discretion. Kindness, words of appreciation, and encouragement were alien to his lips. After studying the principles discussed in this book, this employer sharply altered his philosophy of life. His organization is now inspired with a new loyalty, a new enthusiasm, a new spirit of teamwork. Three hundred and fourteen enemies have been turned into 314 friends. As he proudly said in a speech before the class: "When I used to walk through my establishment, no one greeted me. My employees actually looked the other way when they saw me approaching. But now they are all my friends and even the janitor calls me by my first name."

This employer gained more profit, more leisure, and—what is infinitely more important—he found far more happiness in his business and in his home.

Countless numbers of salespeople have sharply increased their sales by the use of these principles. Many have opened up new accounts—accounts that they had formerly solicited in vain. Executives have been given increased authority, increased pay. One executive reported a large increase in salary because he applied these truths. Another, an executive in the Philadelphia

Gas Works Company, was slated for demotion when he was sixty-five because of his belligerence, because of his inability to lead people skillfully. This training not only saved him from the demotion but brought him a promotion with increased pay.

On innumerable occasions, spouses attending the banquet given at the end of the course have told me that their homes have been much happier since their husbands or wives started this training.

People are frequently astonished at the new results they achieve. It all seems like magic. In some cases, in their enthusiasm, they have telephoned me at my home on Sundays because they couldn't wait forty-eight hours to report their achievements at the regular session of the course.

One man was so stirred by a talk on these principles that he sat far into the night discussing them with other members of the class. At three o'clock in the morning, the others went home. But he was so shaken by a realization of his own mistakes, so inspired by the vista of a new and richer world opening before him, that he was unable to sleep. He didn't sleep that night or the next day or the next night.

Who was he? A naive, untrained individual ready to gush over any new theory that came along? No, far from it. He was a sophisticated, blasé dealer in art, very much the man about town, who spoke three languages fluently and was a graduate of two European universities.

While writing this chapter, I received a letter from a German of the old school, an aristocrat whose forebears had served for generations as professional army officers under the Hohenzollerns. His letter, written from a transatlantic steamer, telling about the application of these principles, rose almost to a religious fervor.

Another man, an old New Yorker, a Harvard graduate, a wealthy man, the owner of a large carpet factory, declared he had learned more in fourteen weeks through this system of training about the fine art of influencing people than he had learned about the same subject during his four years in college. Absurd? Laughable? Fantastic? Of course, you are privileged to dismiss this statement with whatever adjective you wish. I am merely reporting, without comment, a declaration made by a conservative and eminently successful Harvard graduate in a public address to approximately six hundred people at the Yale Club in New York on the evening of Thursday, February 23, 1933.

"Compared to what we ought to be," said the famous Professor William James of Harvard, "compared to what we ought to be, we are only half awake. We are making use of only a small part of our physical and mental resources. Stating the thing broadly, the human individual thus lives far within his limits. He possesses powers of various sorts which he habitually fails to use."

Those powers which you "habitually fail to use"! The sole purpose of this book is to help you discover, develop, and profit by those dormant and unused assets.

"Education," said Dr. John G. Hibben, former president of Princeton University, "is the ability to meet life's situations."

If by the time you have finished reading the first three chapters of this book, if you aren't then a little better equipped to meet life's situations, then I shall consider this book to be a total failure so far as you are concerned.

"For the great aim of education," said Herbert Spencer, "is not knowledge but action."

And this is an action book.

– Dale Carnegie 1936

Nine Suggestions On How To Get The Most Out Of This Book

1. If you wish to get the most out of this book, there is one indispensable requirement, one essential infinitely more important than any rule or technique. Unless you have this one fundamental requisite, a thousand rules on how to study will avail little, and if you do have this cardinal endowment, then you can achieve wonders without reading any suggestions for getting the most out of a book. What is this magic requirement? Just this: a deep, driving desire to learn, a vigorous determination to increase your ability to deal with people. How can you develop such an urge? By constantly reminding yourself how important these principles are to you. Picture to yourself how their mastery will aid you in leading a richer, fuller, happier and more fulfilling life. Say to yourself over and over: "My popularity, my happiness and sense of worth depend to no small extent upon my skill in dealing with people."
2. Read each chapter rapidly at first to get a bird's-eye view of it. You will probably be tempted then to rush on to the next one. But don't, unless you are reading merely for entertainment. But if you are reading because you want to increase your skill in human relations, then go back and reread each chapter thoroughly. In the long run, this will mean saving time and getting results.
3. Stop frequently in your reading to think over what you are reading. Ask yourself just how and when you can apply each suggestion.
4. Read with a crayon, pencil, pen, magic marker or highlighter in your hand. When you come across a suggestion that you feel you can use, draw a line beside it. If it is a four-star suggestion, then underscore every sentence or highlight it, or mark it with "****". Marking and underscoring a book makes it more interesting, and far easier to review rapidly.
5. I knew a woman who had been an office manager for a large insurance concern for fifteen years. Every month, she read all the insurance contracts her company had issued that month. Yes, she read many of the same contracts over month after month, year after year. Why? Because experience had taught her that that was the only way she could keep their

provisions clearly in mind. I once spent almost two years writing a book on public speaking and yet I found I had to keep going back over it from time to time in order to remember what I had written in my own book. The rapidity with which we forget is astonishing. So, if you want to get a real, lasting benefit out of this book, don't imagine that skimming through it once will suffice. After reading it thoroughly, you ought to spend a few hours reviewing it every month. Keep it on your desk in front of you every day. Glance through it often. Keep constantly impressing yourself with the rich possibilities for improvement that still lie in the offing. Remember that the use of these principles can be made habitual only by a constant and vigorous campaign of review and application. There is no other way.

6. Bernard Shaw once remarked, "If you teach a man anything, he will never learn." Shaw was right. Learning is an active process. We learn by doing. So, if you desire to master the principles you are studying in this book, do something about them. Apply these rules at every opportunity. If you don't you will forget them quickly. Only knowledge that is used sticks in your mind. You will probably find it difficult to apply these suggestions all the time. I know because I wrote the book, and yet frequently I found it difficult to apply everything I advocated. For example, when you are displeased, it is much easier to criticize and condemn than it is to try to understand the other person's viewpoint. It is frequently easier to find fault than to find praise. It is more natural to talk about what you want than to talk about what the other person wants and so on. So, as you read this book, remember that you are not merely trying to acquire information. You are attempting to form new habits. Ah yes, you are attempting a new way of life. That will require time and persistence and daily application. So refer to these pages often. Regarding this as a working handbook on human relations; and whenever you are confronted with some specific problem—such as handling a child, winning your spouse to your way of 8 thinking, or satisfying an irritated customer—hesitate about doing the natural thing, the impulsive thing. This is usually wrong. Instead, turn to these pages and review the paragraphs you have underscored. Then try these new ways and watch them achieve magic for you.

7. Offer your spouse, your child or some business associate a dime or a dollar every time he or she catches you violating a certain principle. Make a lively game out of mastering these rules.
8. The president of an important Wall Street bank once described, in a talk before one of my classes, a highly efficient system he used for self-improvement. This man had little formal schooling; yet he had become one of the most important financiers in America, and he confessed that he owed most of his success to the constant application of his homemade system. This is what he does and I'll put it in his own words as accurately as I can remember. "For years I have kept an engagement book showing all the appointments I had during the day. My family never made any plans for me on Saturday night, for the family knew that I devoted a part of each Saturday evening to the illuminating process of self-examination and review and appraisal. After dinner I went off by myself, opened my engagement book, and thought over all the interviews, discussions and meetings that had taken place during the week. I asked myself: 'What mistakes did I make that time?' 'What did I do that was right, and in what way could I have improved my performance?' 'What lessons can I learn from that experience?' "I often found that this weekly review made me very unhappy. I was frequently astonished at my own blunders. Of course, as the years passed, these blunders became less frequent. Sometimes I was inclined to pat myself on the back a little after one of these sessions. This system of self-analysis, self-education, continued year after year, did more for me than any other one thing I have ever attempted. "It helped me improve my ability to make decisions and it aided me enormously in all my contacts with people. I cannot recommend it too highly." Why not use a similar system to check up on your application of the principles discussed in this book? If you do, two things will result. First, you will find yourself engaged in an educational process that is both intriguing and priceless. Second, you will find that your ability to meet and deal with people will grow enormously.
9. You will find at the end of this book several blank pages on which you should record your triumphs in the application of these principles. Be specific. Give names, dates, results. Keeping such a record will inspire you

to greater efforts; and how fascinating these entries will be when you chance upon them some evening years from now!

In order to get the most out of this book:

- Develop a deep, driving desire to master the principles of human relations.
- Read each chapter twice before going on to the next one.
- As you read, stop frequently to ask yourself how you can apply each suggestion.
- Underscore each important idea.
- Review this book each month.
- Apply these principles at every opportunity. Use this volume as a working handbook to help you solve your daily problems.
- Make a lively game out of your learning by offering some friend a dime or a dollar every time he or she catches you violating one of these principles.
- Check up each week on the progress you are making. Ask yourself what mistakes you have made, what improvement, what lessons you have learned for the future.
- Keep notes in the back of this book showing how and when you have applied these principles.

PART ONE

Fundamental Techniques In Handling People

↣ 1 ↢

"IF YOU WANT TO GATHER HONEY, DON'T KICK OVER THE BEEHIVE."

On May 7, 1931, the most sensational manhunt New York City had ever known had come to its climax. After weeks of searching, "Two Gun" Crowley—the killer, the gunman who didn't smoke or drink—was at bay, trapped in his sweetheart's apartment on West End Avenue.

One hundred and fifty policemen and detectives laid siege to his top-floor hideaway. They chopped holes in the roof; they tried to smoke out Crowley, the "cop killer," with teargas. Then they mounted their machine guns on surrounding buildings, and for more than an hour one of New York's fine residential areas reverberated with the crack of pistol fire and the rut-tat-tat of machine guns. Crowley, crouching behind an over-stuffed chair, fired incessantly at the police. Ten thousand excited people watched the battle. Nothing like it has ever been seen before on the sidewalks of New York.

When Crowley was captured, Police Commissioner E. P. Mulrooney declared that the two-gun desperado was one of the most dangerous criminals ever encountered in the history of New York. "He will kill," said the Commissioner, "at the drop of a feather."

But how did "Two Gun" Crowley regard himself? We know, because while the police were firing into his apartment, he wrote a letter addressed "To whom it may concern, " and, as he wrote, the blood flowing from his wounds left a crimson trail on the paper. In this letter Crowley said, "Under my coat is a weary heart, but a kind one—one that would do nobody any harm."

A short time before this, Crowley had been having a necking party with his girlfriend on a country road out on Long Island. Suddenly a policeman walked up to the car and said, "Let me see your license."

Without saying a word, Crowley drew his gun and cut the policeman down with a shower of lead. As the dying officer fell, Crowley leaped out of the car, grabbed the officer's revolver, and fired another bullet into the prostrate body. And that was the killer who said, "Under my coat is a weary heart, but a kind one—one that would do nobody any harm.'

Crowley was sentenced to the electric chair. When he arrived at the death house in Sing Sing, did he say, "This is what I get for killing people"? No, he said, "This is what I get for defending myself."

The point of the story is this: "Two Gun" Crowley didn't blame himself for anything.

Is that an unusual attitude among criminals? If you think so, listen to this:

"I have spent the best years of my life giving people the lighter pleasures, helping them have a good time, and all I get is abuse, the existence of a hunted man."

That's Al Capone speaking. Yes, America's most notorious Public Enemy—the most sinister gang leader who ever shot up Chicago. Capone didn't condemn himself. He actually regarded himself as a public benefactor—an unappreciated and misunderstood public benefactor.

And so did Dutch Schultz before he crumpled up under gangster bullets in Newark. Dutch Schultz, one of New York's most notorious rats, said in a newspaper interview that he was a public benefactor. And he believed it.

I have had some interesting correspondence with Lewis Lawes, who was warden of New York's infamous Sing Sing prison for many years, on this subject, and he declared that "few of the criminals in Sing Sing regard themselves as bad men. They are just as human as you and I. So they rationalize, they explain. They can tell you why they had to crack a safe or be quick on the trigger finger. Most of them attempt by a form of reasoning, fallacious or logical, to justify their anti-social acts even to themselves, consequently stoutly maintaining that they should never have been imprisoned at all."

If Al Capone, "Two Gun" Crowley, Dutch Schultz, and the desperate men and women behind prison walls don't blame themselves for anything—what about the people with whom you and I come in contact?

John Wanamaker, founder of the stores that bear his name, once confessed, "I learned thirty years ago that it is foolish to scold. I have enough trouble overcoming my own limitations without fretting over the fact that God has not seen fit to distribute evenly the gift of intelligence."

Wanamaker learned this lesson early, but I personally had to blunder through this old world for a third of a century before it even began to dawn upon me that ninety-nine times out of a hundred, people don't criticize themselves for anything, no matter how wrong it may be.

Criticism is futile because it puts a person on the defensive and usually makes him strive to justify himself. Criticism is dangerous, because it wounds a person's precious pride, hurts his sense of importance, and arouses resentment.

B. F. Skinner, the world-famous psychologist, proved through his experiments that an animal rewarded for good behavior will learn much more rapidly and retain what it learns far more effectively than an animal punished for bad behavior. Later studies have shown that the same applies to humans. By criticizing, we do not make lasting changes and often incur resentment.

Hans Selye, another great psychologist, said, "As much as we thirst for approval, we dread condemnation."

The resentment that criticism engenders can demoralize employees, family members and friends, and still not correct the situation that has been condemned.

George B. Johnston of Enid, Oklahoma, is the safety coordinator for an engineering company. One of his responsibilities is to see that employees wear their hard hats whenever they are on the job in the field. He reported that whenever he came across workers who were not wearing hard hats, he would tell them with a lot of authority of the regulation and that they must comply. As a result he would get sullen acceptance, and often after he left, the workers would remove the hats.

He decided to try a different approach. The next time he found some of the workers not wearing their hard hat, he asked if the hats were uncomfortable or did not fit properly. Then he reminded the men in a pleasant tone of voice that the hat was designed to protect them from injury and suggested that it should always be worn on the job. The result was increased compliance with the regulation with no resentment or emotional upset.

You will find examples of the futility of criticism bristling on a thousand pages of history, Take, for example, the famous quarrel between Theodore Roosevelt and President Taft—a quarrel that split the Republican party, put Woodrow Wilson in the White House, and wrote bold, luminous lines across the First World War and altered the flow of history. Let's review the facts quickly. When Theodore Roosevelt stepped out of the White House in 1908, he supported Taft, who was elected President. Then Theodore Roosevelt went off to Africa to shoot lions. When he returned, he exploded. He denounced Taft for his conservatism, tried to secure the nomination for a third term himself, formed the Bull Moose party, and all but demolished the G.O.P. In the election that followed, William Howard Taft and the Republican party carried only two states—Vermont and Utah. The most disastrous defeat the party had ever known.

Theodore Roosevelt blamed Taft, but did President Taft blame himself? Of course not. With tears in his eyes, Taft said: "I don't see how I could have done any differently from what I have."

Who was to blame? Roosevelt or Taft? Frankly, I don't know, and I don't care. The point I am trying to make is that all of Theodore Roosevelt's criticism didn't persuade Taft that he was wrong. It merely made Taft strive to justify himself and to reiterate with tears in his eyes: "I don't see how I could have done any differently from what I have."

Or, take the Teapot Dome oil scandal. It kept the newspapers ringing with indignation in the early 1920s. It rocked the nation! Within the memory of living men, nothing like it had ever happened before in American public life. Here are the bare facts of the scandal: Albert B. Fall, secretary of the interior in Harding's cabinet, was entrusted with the leasing of government oil reserves at Elk Hill and Teapot Dome—oil reserves that had been set aside for the future use of the Navy. Did secretary Fall permit competitive bidding? No sir. He handed the fat, juicy contract outright to his friend Edward L. Doheny. And what did Doheny do? He gave Secretary Fall what he was pleased to call a "loan" of one hundred thousand dollars. Then, in a high-handed manner, Secretary Fall ordered United States Marines into the district to drive off competitors whose adjacent wells were sapping oil out of the Elk Hill reserves. These competitors, driven off their ground at the ends of guns and bayonets, rushed into court—and blew the lid off the Teapot Dome scandal. A stench arose so vile that it ruined the Harding Administration, nauseated an entire nation, threatened to wreck the Republican party, and put Albert B. Fall behind prison bars.

Fall was condemned viciously—condemned as few men in public life have ever been. Did he repent? Never! Years later Herbert Hoover intimated in a public speech that President Harding's death had been due to mental anxiety and worry because a friend had betrayed him. When Mrs. Fall heard that, she sprang from her chair, she wept, she shook her fists at fate and screamed, "What! Harding betrayed by Fall? No! My husband never betrayed anyone. This whole house full of gold would not tempt my husband to do wrong. He is the one who has been betrayed and led to the slaughter and crucified."

There you are; human nature in action, wrongdoers, blaming everybody but themselves. We are all like that. So when you and I are tempted to criticize someone tomorrow, let's remember Al Capone, "Two Gun" Crowley and Albert Fall. Let's realize that criticisms are like homing pigeons. They always return home. Let's realize that the person we are going to correct and condemn will probably justify himself or herself, and condemn us in return; or, like the gentle Taft, will say, "I don't see how I could have done any differently from what I have."

On the morning of April 15, 1865, Abraham Lincoln lay dying in a hall bedroom of a cheap lodging house directly across the street from Ford's Theater, where John Wilkes Booth had shot him. Lincoln's long body lay stretched diagonally across a sagging bed that was too short for him. A cheap reproduction of Rosa Bonheur's famous painting The Horse Fair hung above the bed, and a dismal gas jet flickered yellow light.

As Lincoln lay dying, Secretary of War Stanton said, "There lies the most perfect ruler of men that the world has ever seen."

What was the secret of Lincoln's success in dealing with people? I studied the life of Abraham Lincoln for ten years and devoted all of three years to writing and rewriting a book entitled Lincoln the Unknown. I believe I have made as detailed and exhaustive a study of Lincoln's personality and home life as it is possible for any being to make. I made a special study of Lincoln's method of dealing with people. Did he indulge in criticism? Oh, yes. As a young man in the Pigeon Creek Valley of Indiana, he not only criticized but he wrote letters and poems ridiculing people and dropped these letters on the country roads where they were sure to be found. One of these letters aroused resentments that burned for a lifetime.

Even after Lincoln had become a practicing lawyer in Springfield, Illinois, he attacked his opponents openly in letters published in the newspapers. But he did this just once too often.

In the autumn of 1842 he ridiculed a vain, pugnacious politician by the name of James Shields. Lincoln lambasted him through an anonymous letter published in Springfield Journal. The town roared with laughter. Shields, sensitive and proud, boiled with indignation. He found out who wrote the letter, leaped on his horse, started after Lincoln, and challenged him to fight a duel. Lincoln didn't want to fight. He was opposed to dueling, but he couldn't get out of it and save his honor. He was given the choice of weapons. Since he had very long arms, he chose cavalry broadswords and took lessons in sword fighting from a West Point graduate; and, on the appointed day, he and Shields met on a sandbar in the Mississippi River, prepared to fight to the death; but, at the last minute, their seconds interrupted and stopped the duel.

That was the most lurid personal incident in Lincoln's life. It taught him an invaluable lesson in the art of dealing with people. Never again did he write an insulting letter. Never again did he ridicule anyone. And from that time on, he almost never criticized anybody for anything.

Time after time, during the Civil War, Lincoln put a new general at the head of the Army of the Potomac, and each one in turn—McClellan, Pope, Burnside, Hooker, Meade—blundered tragically and drove Lincoln to pacing the floor in despair. Half the nation savagely condemned these incompetent generals, but Lincoln, "with malice toward none, with charity for all," held his peace. One of his favorite quotations was "Judge not, that ye be not judged."

And when Mrs. Lincoln and others spoke harshly of the southern people, Lincoln replied, "Don't criticize them; they are just what we would be under similar circumstances."

Yet if any man ever had occasion to criticize, surely it was Lincoln. Let's take just one illustration:

The Battle of Gettysburg was fought during the first three days of July 1863. During the night of July 4, Lee began to retreat southward while storm clouds deluged the country with rain. When Lee reached the Potomac with his defeated army, he found a swollen, impassable river in front of him, and a victorious Union Army behind him. Lee was in a trap. He couldn't escape. Lincoln saw that. Here was a golden, heaven-sent opportunity—the opportunity to capture Lee's army and end the war immediately. So, with a surge of high hope, Lincoln ordered Meade not to call a council of war but to attack Lee immediately. Lincoln telegraphed his orders and then sent a special messenger to Meade demanding immediate action.

And what did General Meade do? He did the very opposite of what he was told to do. He called a council of war in direct violation of Lincoln's orders. He hesitated. He procrastinated. He telegraphed all manner of excuses. He refused point-blank to attack Lee. Finally the waters receded and Lee escaped over the Potomac with his forces.

Lincoln was furious, " What does this mean?" Lincoln cried to his son Robert. "Great God! What does this mean? We had them within our grasp, and had only to stretch forth our hands and they were ours; yet nothing that I could say or do could make the army move. Under the circumstances, almost any general could have defeated Lee. If I had gone up there, I could have whipped him myself."

In bitter disappointment, Lincoln sat down and wrote Meade this letter. And remember, at this period of his life Lincoln was extremely conservative and restrained in his phraseology. So this letter coming from Lincoln in 1863 was tantamount to the severest rebuke.

"My dear General,

I do not believe you appreciate the magnitude of the misfortune involved in Lee's escape. He was within our easy grasp, and to have closed upon him would, in connection with our other late successes, have ended the war. As it is, the war will be prolonged indefinitely. If you could not safely attack Lee last Monday, how can you possibly do so south of the river, when you can take with you very few—no more than two-thirds of the force you then had in hand? It would be unreasonable to expect and I do not expect that you can now affect much. Your golden opportunity is gone, and I am distressed immeasurably because of it."

What do you suppose Meade did when he read the letter?

Meade never saw that letter. Lincoln never mailed it. It was found among his papers after his death.

My guess is—and this is only a guess—that after writing that letter, Lincoln looked out of the window and said to himself, "Just a minute. Maybe I ought not to be so hasty. It is easy enough for me to sit here in the quiet of the White House and order Meade to attack; but if I had been up at Gettysburg, and if I had seen as much blood as Meade has seen during the last week, and if my ears had been pierced with the screams and shrieks of the wounded and dying, maybe I wouldn't be so anxious to attack either. If I had Meade's timid temperament, perhaps I would have done just what he had done. Anyhow, it is water under the bridge now. If I send this letter, it will relieve my feelings, but it will make Meade try to justify himself. It will make him condemn me. It will arouse hard feelings, impair all his further usefulness as a commander, and perhaps force him to resign from the army."

So, as I have already said, Lincoln put the letter aside, for he had learned by bitter experience that sharp criticisms and rebukes almost invariably end in futility.

Theodore Roosevelt said that when he, as President, was confronted with a perplexing problem, he used to lean back and look up at a large painting of Lincoln which hung above his desk in the White House and ask himself, "What would Lincoln do if he were in my shoes? How would he solve this problem?"

The next time we are tempted to admonish somebody, let's pull a five-dollar bill out of our pocket, look at Lincoln's picture on the bill, and ask. "How would Lincoln handle this problem if he had it?"

Mark Twain lost his temper occasionally and wrote letters that turned the Paper brown. For example, he once wrote to a man who had aroused his ire: "The thing for you is a burial permit. You have only to speak and I will see that you get it." On another occasion he wrote to an editor about a proofreader's attempts to "improve my spelling and punctuation." He ordered, "Set the matter according to my copy hereafter and see that the proofreader retains his suggestions in the mush of his decayed brain."

The writing of these stinging letters made Mark Twain feel better. They allowed him to blow off steam, and the letters didn't do any real harm, because Mark's wife secretly lifted them out of the mail. They were never sent.

Do you know someone you would like to change and regulate and improve? Good! That is fine. I am all in favor of it, but why not begin with yourself? From a purely selfish standpoint, that is a lot more profitable than trying to improve others—yes, and a lot less dangerous.

"Don't complain about the snow on your neighbor's roof," said Confucius, "when your own doorstep is unclean."

When I was still young and trying hard to impress people, I wrote a foolish letter to Richard Harding Davis, an author who once loomed large on the literary horizon of America. I was preparing a magazine article about authors, and I asked Davis to tell me about his method of work. A few weeks earlier, I had received a letter from someone with this notation at the bottom: "Dictated but not read." I was quite impressed. I felt that the writer must be very big and busy and important. I wasn't the slightest bit busy, but I was eager to make an impression on Richard Harding Davis, so I ended my short note with the words: "Dictated but not read."

He never bothered to answer the letter. He simply returned it to me with this scribbled across the bottom: "Your bad manners are exceeded only by your bad manners." True, I had blundered, and perhaps I deserved this rebuke. But, being human, I resented it. I resented it so sharply that when I read of the death of Richard Harding Davis ten years later, the one thought that still persisted in my mind—I am ashamed to admit— was the hurt he had given me.

If you and I want to stir up a resentment tomorrow that may rankle across the decades and endure until death, just let us indulge in a little stinging criticism, no matter how certain we are that it is justified.

When dealing with people, let us remember we are not dealing with creatures of logic. We are dealing with creatures of emotion, creatures bristling with prejudices and motivated by pride and vanity.

Bitter criticism caused the sensitive Thomas Hardy, one of the finest novelists ever to enrich English literature, to give up forever the writing of fiction. Criticism drove Thomas Chatterton, the English poet, to suicide.

Benjamin Franklin, tactless in his youth, became so diplomatic, so adroit at handling people, that he was made American Ambassador to France. The secret of his success? "I will speak ill of no man," he said, "and speak all the good I know of everybody."

Any fool can criticize, condemn and complain, and most fools do.

But it takes character and self-control to be understanding and forgiving.

"A great man shows his greatness," said Carlyle, "by the way he treats little men."

Bob Hoover, a famous test pilot and frequent performer at air shows, was returning to his home in Los Angeles from an air show in San Diego. As described in the magazine Flight Operations, at three hundred feet in the air, both engines suddenly stopped. By deft maneuvering he managed to land the plane, but it was badly damaged although nobody was hurt.

Hoover's first act after the emergency landing was to inspect the airplane's fuel. Just as he suspected, the World War II propeller plane he had been flying had been fueled with jet fuel rather than gasoline.

Upon returning to the airport, he asked to see the mechanic who had serviced his airplane. The young man was sick with the agony of his mistake. Tears streamed down his face as Hoover approached. He had just caused the loss of a very expensive plane and could have caused the loss of three lives as well.

You can imagine Hoover's anger. One could anticipate the tongue-lashing that this proud and precise pilot would unleash for that carelessness. But Hoover didn't scold the mechanic; he didn't even criticize him. Instead, he put his big arm around the man's shoulder and said, "To show you I'm sure that you'll never do this again, I want you to service my F-51 tomorrow."

Often parents are tempted to criticize their children. You would expect me to say "don't." But I will not, I am merely going to say, "Before you criticize them, read one of the classics of American journalism, 'Father Forgets'." It originally appeared as an editorial in the People's Home Journal. We are reprinting it here with the author's permission, as condensed in the Reader's Digest.

"Father Forgets" is one of those little pieces which—dashed of in a moment of sincere feeling—strikes an echoing chord in so many readers as to become a perennial reprint favorite. Since its first appearance, "Father Forgets" has been reproduced, writes the author, W. Livingston

Larned, "in hundreds of magazines and house organs, and in newspapers the country over. It has been reprinted almost as extensively in many foreign languages. I have given personal permission to thousands who wished to read it from school, church, and lecture platforms. It has been 'on the air' on countless occasions and programs. Oddly enough, college periodicals have used it, and high-school magazines. Sometimes a little piece seems mysteriously to 'click'. This one certainly did."

FATHER FORGETS
W. Livingston Larned

Listen, son: I am saying this as you lie asleep, one little paw crumpled under your cheek and the blond curls stickily wet on your damp forehead. I have stolen into your room alone. Just a few minutes ago, as I sat reading my paper in the library, a stifling wave of remorse swept over me. Guiltily I came to your bedside.

There are the things I was thinking, son: I had been cross to you. I scolded you as you were dressing for school because you gave your face merely a dab with a towel. I took you to task for not cleaning your shoes. I called out angrily when you threw some of your things on the floor.

At breakfast I found fault, too. You spilled things. You gulped down your food. You put your elbows on the table. You spread butter too thick on your bread. And as you started off to play and I made for my train, you turned and waved a hand and called, "Goodbye, Daddy!" and I frowned, and said in reply, "Hold your shoulders back!"

Then it began all over again in the late afternoon. As I came up the road I spied you, down on your knees, playing marbles. There were holes in your stockings. I humiliated you before your boyfriends by marching you ahead of me to the house. Stockings were expensive, and if you had to buy them you would be more careful! Imagine that, son, from a father!

Do you remember, later, when I was reading in the library, how you came in timidly, with a sort of hurt look in your eyes? When I glanced up over my paper, impatient at the interruption, you hesitated at the door. "What is it you want?" I snapped.

You said nothing, but ran across in one tempestuous plunge, and threw your arms around my neck and kissed me, and your small arms tightened with an affection that God had set blooming in your heart and which even neglect could not wither. And then you were gone, pattering up the stairs.

Well, son, it was shortly afterwards that my paper slipped from my hands and a terrible sickening fear came over me. What has habit been doing to me? The habit of finding fault, of reprimanding—this was my reward to you for being a boy. It was not that I did not love you; it was that I expected too much of youth. I was measuring you by the yardstick of my own years.

And there was so much that was good and fine and true in your character. The little heart of you was as big as the dawn itself over the wide hills. This was shown by your spontaneous impulse to rush in and kiss me goodnight. Nothing else matters tonight, son. I have come to your bedside in the darkness, and I have knelt there, ashamed!

It is a feeble atonement; I know you would not understand these things if I told them to you during your waking hours. But tomorrow I will be a real daddy! I will chum with you, and suffer when you suffer, and laugh when you laugh. I will bite my tongue when impatient words come. I will keep saying as if it were a ritual: "He is nothing but a boy—a little boy!"

I am afraid I have visualized you as a man. Yet as I see you now, son, crumpled and weary in your cot, I see that you are still a baby. Yesterday you were in your mother's arms, your head on her shoulder. I have asked too much, too much.

Instead of condemning people, let's try to understand them. Let's try to figure out why they do what they do. That's a lot more profitable and intriguing than criticism, and it breeds sympathy, tolerance and kindness. "To know all is to forgive all."

As Dr. Johnson said, "God himself, sir, does not propose to judge man until the end of his days."

Why should you and I?

⟹ PRINCIPLE 1 ⟸

Don't criticize, condemn or complain

↣ 2 ↢

"THE BIG SECRET OF DEALING WITH PEOPLE."

There is only one way under high heaven to get anybody to do anything. Did you ever stop to think of that? Yes, just one way. And that is by making the other person want to do it.

Remember, there is no other way.

Of course, you can make someone want to give you his watch by sticking a revolver in his ribs. You can make your employees give you cooperation—until your back is turned—by threatening to fire them. You can make a child do what you want it to do by a whip or a threat. But these crude methods have sharply undesirable repercussions.

The only way I can get you to do anything is by giving you what you want.

What do you want?

Sigmund Freud said that everything you and I do springs from two motives: the sex urge and the desire to be great.

John Dewey, one of America's most profound philosophers, phrased it a bit differently. Dr. Dewey said that the deepest urge in human nature is "the desire to be important." Remember that phrase: "the desire to be important." It is significant. You are going to hear a lot about it in this book.

What do you want? Not many things, but the few that you do wish, you crave with an insistence that will not be denied. Some of the things most people want include:

1. *Health and the preservation of life.*
2. *Food.*
3. *Sleep.*
4. *Money and the things money will buy.*
5. *Life in the hereafter.*

6. *Sexual gratification.*
7. *The well-being of our children.*
8. *A feeling of importance.*

Almost all these wants are usually gratified—all except one. But there is one longing—almost as deep, almost as imperious, as the desire for food or sleep—which is seldom gratified. It is what Freud calls "the desire to be great." It is what Dewey calls the "desire to be important."

Lincoln once began a letter saying, "Everybody likes a compliment." William James said, "The deepest principle in human nature is the craving to be appreciated." He didn't speak, mind you, of the "wish" or the "desire" or the "longing" to be appreciated. He said the "craving" to be appreciated.

Here is a gnawing and unfaltering human hunger, and the rare individual who honestly satisfies this heart hunger will hold people in the palm of his or her hand and "even the undertaker will be sorry when he dies."

The desire for a feeling of importance is one of the chief distinguishing differences between mankind and the animals. To illustrate: When I was a farm boy out in Missouri, my father bred fine Duroc-Jersey hogs and pedigreed white-faced cattle. We used to exhibit our hogs and white-faced cattle at the country fairs and livestock shows throughout the Middle West. We won first prizes by the score. My father pinned his blue ribbons on a sheet of white muslin, and when friends or visitors came to the house, he would get out the long sheet of muslin. He would hold one end and I would hold the other while he exhibited the blue ribbons.

The hogs didn't care about the ribbons they had won. But Father did. These prizes gave him a feeling of importance.

If our ancestors hadn't had this flaming urge for a feeling of importance, civilization would have been impossible. Without it, we should have been just about like animals.

It was this desire for a feeling of importance that led an uneducated, poverty-stricken grocery clerk to study some law books he found in the bottom of a barrel of household plunder that he had bought for fifty cents. You have probably heard of this grocery clerk. His name was Lincoln.

It was this desire for a feeling of importance that inspired Dickens to write his immortal novels. This desire inspired Sir Christopher Wren to design his symphonies in stone. This desire made Rockefeller amass millions that he never spent. And this same desire made the richest family in your town build a house far too large for its requirements.

This desire makes you want to wear the latest styles, drive the latest cars, and talk about your brilliant children.

It is this desire that lures many boys and girls into joining gangs and engaging in criminal activities. The average young criminal, according to E. P. Mulrooney, one-time police commissioner of New York, is filled with ego, and his first request after arrest is for those lurid newspapers that make him out a hero. The disagreeable prospect of serving time seems remote so long as he can gloat over his likeness sharing space with pictures of sports figures, movie and TV stars, and politicians.

If you tell me how you get your feeling of importance, I'll tell you what you are. That determines your character. That is the most significant thing about you. For example, John D. Rockefeller got his feeling of importance by giving money to erect a modern hospital in Peking, China, to care for millions of poor people whom he had never seen and never would see. Dillinger, on the other hand, got his feeling of importance by being a bandit, a bank robber, and killer. When the FBI agents were hunting him, he dashed into a farmhouse up in Minnesota and said, "I'm Dillinger!" He was proud of the fact that he was Public Enemy Number One. "I'm not going to hurt you, but I'm Dillinger!" he said.

Yes, the one significant difference between Dillinger and Rockefeller is how they got their feeling of importance.

History sparkles with amusing examples of famous people struggling for a feeling of importance. Even George Washington wanted to be called "His Mightiness, the President of the United States"; and Columbus pleaded for the title "Admiral of the Ocean and Viceroy of India." Catherine the Great refused to open letters that were not addressed to "Her Imperial Majesty"; and Mrs. Lincoln, in the White House, turned upon Mrs. Grant like a tigress and shouted, "How dare you be seated in my presence until I invite you!"

Our millionaires helped finance Admiral Byrd's expedition to the Antarctic in 1928 with the understanding that ranges of icy mountains would be named after them; and Victor Hugo aspired to have nothing less than the city of Paris renamed in his honor. Even Shakespeare, mightiest of the mighty, tried to add luster to his name by procuring a coat of arms for his family.

People sometimes become invalids in order to win sympathy and attention, and get a feeling of importance. For example, take Mrs. McKinley. She got a feeling of importance by forcing her husband, the President of the United States, to neglect important affairs of state while he reclined on the bed beside her for hours at a time, his arm about her, soothing her to sleep. She fed her gnawing desire for attention by insisting that he remain with her while she was having her teeth fixed, and once created a stormy scene when he had to leave her alone with the dentist while he kept an appointment with John Hay, his secretary of state.

The writer Mary Roberts Rinehart once told me of a bright, vigorous young woman who became an invalid in order to get a feeling of importance. "One day," said Mrs. Rinehart, "this woman had been obliged to face something, her age perhaps. The lonely years were stretching ahead and there was little left for her to anticipate.

"She took to her bed; and for ten years her old mother traveled to the third floor and back, carrying trays, nursing her. Then one day the old mother, weary with service, lay down and died. For some weeks, the invalid languished; then she got up, put on her clothing, and resumed living again."

Some authorities declare that people may actually go insane in order to find, in the dreamland of insanity, the feeling of importance that has been denied them in the harsh world of reality. There are more patients suffering from mental diseases in the United States than from all other diseases combined.

What is the cause of insanity?

Nobody can answer such a sweeping question, but we know that certain diseases, such as syphilis, break down and destroy the brain cells and result in insanity. In fact, about one-half of all mental diseases can be attributed to such physical causes as brain lesions, alcohol, toxins, and injuries. But the other half—and this is the appalling part of the story—the other half of the people who go insane apparently have nothing organically wrong with their brain cells. In post-mortem examinations, when their brain tissues are studied under the highest-powered microscopes, these tissues are found to be apparently just as healthy as yours and mine.

Why do these people go insane?

I put that question to the head physician of one of our most important psychiatric hospitals. This doctor, who has received the highest honors and the most coveted awards for his knowledge of this subject, told me frankly that he didn't know why people went insane. Nobody knows for sure. But he did say that many people who go insane find in insanity a feeling of importance that they were unable to achieve in the world of reality. Then he told me this story:

"I have a patient right now whose marriage proved to be a tragedy. She wanted love, sexual gratification, children, and social prestige, but life blasted all her hopes. Her husband didn't love her. He refused even to eat with her and forced her to serve his meals in his room upstairs. She had no children, no social standing. She went insane; and, in her imagination, she divorced her husband and resumed her maiden name. She now believes she has married into the English aristocracy, and she insists on being called Lady Smith.

"And as for children, she imagines now that she has had a new child every night. Each time I call on her she says, 'Doctor, I had a baby last night.'"

Life once wrecked all her dream ships on the sharp rocks of reality; but in the sunny, fantasy isles of insanity, all her barkentines race into port with canvas billowing and winds singing through the masts.

"Tragic? Oh, I don't know. Her physician said to me, 'If I could stretch out my hand and restore her sanity, I wouldn't do it. She's much happier as she is.'"

If some people are so hungry for a feeling of importance that they actually go insane to get it, imagine what miracle you and I can achieve by giving people honest appreciation for this side of insanity.

One of the first people in American business to be paid a salary of over a million dollars a year (when there was no income tax and a person earning fifty dollars a week was considered well-off) was Charles Schwab, who had been picked by Andrew Carnegie to become the first president of the newly formed United States Steel Company in 1921, when he was only thirty-eight years old (Schwab later left U.S. Steel to take over the then-troubled Bethlehem Steel Company, and he rebuilt it into one of the most profitable companies in America).

Why did Andrew Carnegie pay a million dollars a year, or more than three thousand dollars a day, to Charles Schwab? Why? Because Schwab was a genius? No. Because he knew more about the manufacture of steel than other people? Nonsense. Charles Schwab told me himself that he had many men working for him who knew more about the manufacture of steel than he did.

Schwab says that he was paid this salary largely because of his ability to deal with people. I asked him how he did it. Here is his secret set down in his own words—words that ought to be cast in eternal bronze and hung in every home and school, every shop and office in the land—words that children ought to memorize instead of wasting their time memorizing the conjugation of Latin verbs or the amount of the annual rainfall in Brazil—words that will all but transform your life and mine if we will only live them:

"I consider my ability to arouse enthusiasm among my people," said Schwab, "the greatest asset I possess, and the way to develop the best that is in a person is by appreciation and encouragement.

"There is nothing else that so kills the ambitions of a person as criticism from superiors. I never criticize anyone. I believe in giving a person incentive to work. So I am anxious to praise but loath to find fault. If I like anything, I am hearty in my approbation and lavish in my praise."

That is what Schwab did. But what do average people do? The exact opposite. If they don't like a thing, they bawl out their subordinates; if they do like it, they say nothing. As the old couplet says: "Once I did bad and that I heard ever/Twice I did good, but that I heard never."

"In my wide association in life, meeting with many and great people in various parts of the world," Schwab declared, "I have yet to find the person, however great or exalted his station, who did not do better work and put forth greater effort under a spirit of approval than he would ever do under a spirit of criticism."

That he said, frankly, was one of the outstanding reasons for the phenomenal success of Andrew Carnegie. Carnegie praised his associates publicly as well as privately.

Carnegie wanted to praise his assistants even on his tombstone. He wrote an epitaph for himself which read: "Here lies one who knew how to get around men who were cleverer than himself."

Sincere appreciation was one of the secrets of the first John D. Rockefeller's success in handling men. For example, when one of his partners, Edward T. Bedford, lost a million dollars for the firm by a bad buy in South America, John D. might have criticized; but he knew Bedford had done his best, and the incident was closed. So Rockefeller found something to praise; he congratulated Bedford because he had been able to save 60 percent of the money he had invested. "That's splendid," said Rockefeller. "We don't always do as well as that upstairs."

I have among my clippings a story that I know never happened, but it illustrates a truth, so I'll repeat it: According to this silly story, a farmwoman, at the end of a heavy day's work, set before her menfolk a heaping pile of hay. And when they indignantly demanded whether she had gone crazy, she replied: "Why, how did I know you'd notice? I've been cooking for you men for the last twenty years and in all that time I ain't heard no word to let me know you weren't just eating hay."

When a study was made a few years ago on runaway wives, what do you think was discovered to be the main reason wives ran away? It was "lack of appreciation." And I'd bet that a similar study made of runaway husbands would come out the same way. We often take our spouses so much for granted that we never let them know we appreciate them.

A member of one of our classes told of a request made by his wife. She and a group of other women in her church were involved in a self-improvement program. She asked her husband to help her by listing six things he believed she could do to help herself become a better wife. He reported to the class, "I was surprised by such a request. Frankly, it would have been easy for me to list six things I would like to change about her—my heavens. She could have listed a thousand things she would like to change about me—but I didn't. I said to her, 'Let me think about it and give you an answer in the morning.'

"The next morning I got up very early and called the florist and had them send six red roses to my wife with a note saying: 'I can't think of six things I would like to change about you. I love you the way you are.'

"When I arrived at home that evening, who do you think greeted me at the door? That's right. My wife! She was almost in tears. Needless to say, I was extremely glad I had not criticized her as she had requested.

"The following Sunday at church, after she had reported the results of her assignment, several women with whom she had been studying came up to me and said, 'That was the most considerate thing I have ever heard.' It was then I realized the power of appreciation."

Florenz Ziegfeld, the most spectacular producer who ever dazzled Broadway, gained his reputation by his subtle ability to "glorify the American girl." Time after time, he took drab little creatures that no one ever looked at twice and transformed them on the stage into glamorous visions of mystery and seduction. Knowing the value of appreciation and confidence, he made women feel beautiful by the sheer power of his gallantry and consideration. He was practical: he raised the salary of chorus girls from thirty dollars a week to as high as one hundred and seventy-five. And he was also chivalrous; on opening night at the Follies, he sent telegrams to the stars in the cast, and he deluged every chorus girl in the show with American Beauty roses.

I once succumbed to the fad of fasting and went for six days and nights without eating. It wasn't difficult. I was less hungry at the end of the sixth day than I was at the end of the second. Yet I know, as you know, people who would think they had committed a crime if they let their families or employees go for six days without food; but they will let them go for six days, and six weeks, and sometimes sixty years without giving them the hearty appreciation that they crave almost as much as they crave food.

When Alfred Lunt, one of the great actors of his time, played the leading role in Reunion in Vienna, he said, "There is nothing I need so much as nourishment for my self-esteem."

We nourish the bodies of our children and friends and employees, but how seldom do we nourish their self-esteem? We provide them with roast beef and potatoes to build energy, but we neglect to give them kind words of appreciation that would sing in their memories for years like the music of the morning stars.

Paul Harvey, in one of his radio broadcasts, "The Rest of the Story," told how showing sincere appreciation could change a person's life. He reported that years ago a teacher in Detroit asked Stevie Morris to help her find a mouse that was lost in the classroom. You see, she appreciated the fact that nature had given Stevie something no one else in the room had. Nature had given Stevie a remarkable pair of ears to compensate for his blind eyes. But this was really the first time Stevie had been shown appreciation for those talented ears. Now, years later, he says that this act of appreciation was the beginning of a new life. You see, from that time on he developed his gift of hearing and went on to become, under the stage name of Stevie Wonder, one of the great pop singers and songwriters of the seventies.

Some readers are saying right now as they read these lines, "Oh, phooey! Flattery! Bear oil! I've tried that stuff. It doesn't work—not with intelligent people."

Of course, flattery seldom works with discerning people. It is shallow, selfish, and insincere. It ought to fail and it usually does. True, some people are so hungry, so thirsty, for appreciation that they will swallow anything, just as a starving man will eat grass and fishworms.

Even Queen Victoria was susceptible to flattery. Prime Minister Benjamin Disraeli confessed that he put it on thick in dealing with the Queen. To use his exact words, he said he "spread it on with a trowel." But Disraeli was one of the most polished, deft, and adroit men who ever ruled the far-flung British Empire. He was a genius in his line. What would work for him wouldn't necessarily work for you and me. In the long run, flattery will do you more harm than good. Flattery is counterfeit, and like counterfeit money, it will eventually get you into trouble if you pass it to someone else.

The difference between appreciation and flattery? That is simple. One is sincere and the other insincere. One comes from the heart out; the other from the teeth out. One is unselfish; the other selfish. One is universally admired; the other universally condemned.

I recently saw a bust of Mexican hero General Alvaro Obregon in the Chapultepec palace in Mexico City. Below the bust are carved these wise words from General Obregon's philosophy: "Don't be afraid of enemies who attack you. Be afraid of the friends who flatter you."

No! No! No! I am not suggesting flattery! Far from it. I'm talking about a new way of life. Let me repeat. I am talking about a new way of life.

King George V had a set of six maxims displayed on the walls of his study at Buckingham Palace. One of these maxims said: "Teach me neither to proffer nor receive cheap praise." That's all flattery is—cheap praise. I once read a definition of flattery that may be worth repeating:

"Flattery is telling the other person precisely what he thinks about himself."

"Use what language you will," said Ralph Waldo Emerson, "you can never say anything but what you are."

If all we had to do was flatter, everybody would catch on and we should all be experts in human relations.

When we are not engaged in thinking about some definite problem, we usually spend about 95 percent of our time thinking about ourselves. Now, if we stop thinking about ourselves for a while and begin to think of the other person's good points, we won't have to resort to flattery so cheap and false that it can be spotted almost before it is out of our mouth.

One of the most neglected virtues of our daily existence is appreciation. Somehow, we neglect to praise our son or daughter when he or she brings home a good report card, and we fail to encourage our children when they first succeed in baking a cake or building a birdhouse.

Nothing pleases children more than this kind of parental interest and approval.

The next time you enjoy filet mignon at the club, send word to the chef that it was excellently prepared, and when a tired salesperson shows you unusual courtesy, please mention it.

Every minister, lecturer, and public speaker knows the discouragement of pouring himself or herself out to an audience and not receiving a single ripple of appreciative comment. What applies to professionals applies doubly to workers in offices, shops, and factories and our families and friends. In our interpersonal relations we should never forget that all our associates are human beings and hunger for appreciation. It is the legal tender that all souls enjoy.

Try leaving a friendly trail of little sparks of gratitude on your daily trips. You will be surprised how they will set small flames of friendship that will be rose beacons on your next visit.

Pamela Dunham of New Fairfield, Connecticut, had among her responsibilities on her job the supervision of a janitor who was doing a very poor job. The other employees would jeer at him and litter the hallways to show him what a bad job he was doing. It was so bad, productive time was being lost in the shop.

Without success, Pam tried various ways to motivate this person. She noticed that occasionally he did a particularly good piece of work. She made a point to praise him for it in front of the other people. Each day the job he did all around got better, and pretty soon he started doing all his work efficiently. Now he does an excellent job and other people give him appreciation and recognition. Honest appreciation got results where criticism and ridicule failed.

Hurting people not only does not change them, it is never called for. There is an old saying that I have cut out and pasted on my mirror where I cannot help but see it every day:

> I shall pass this way but once; any good, therefore, that I can do or any kindness that I can show to any human being, let me do it now. Let me not defer nor neglect it, for I shall not pass this way again.

"Every man I meet is my superior in some way. In that, I learn of him," said Emerson.

If that was true of Emerson, isn't it likely to be a thousand times more true of you and me? Let's cease thinking of our accomplishments, our wants. Let's try to figure out the other person's good points. Then forget flattery. Give honest, sincere appreciation. Be "hearty in your approbation and lavish in your praise," and people will cherish your words and treasure them and repeat them over a lifetime—repeat them years after you have forgotten them.

⇒ PRINCIPLE 2 ⇐

Don't criticize, condemn or complain.

↣ 3 ↢

"HE WHO CAN DO THIS HAS THE WHOLE WORLD WITH HIM. HE WHO CANNOT WALK A LONELY WAY."

I often went fishing in Maine during the summer. Personally I am very fond of strawberries and cream, but I have found that for some strange reason, fish prefer worms. So when I went fishing, I didn't think about what I wanted. I thought about what they wanted. I didn't bait the hook with strawberries and cream. Rather, I dangled a worm or a grasshopper in front of the fish and said, "Wouldn't you like to have that?"

Why not use the same common sense when fishing for people?

That is what Lloyd George, Great Britain's Prime Minister during World War I, did. When someone asked him how he managed to stay in power after the other wartime leaders—Wilson, Orlando, and Clemenceau—had been forgotten, he replied that if his staying on top might be attributed to any one thing, it would be to his having learned that it was necessary to bait the hook to suit the fish.

Why talk about what we want? That is childish. Absurd. Of course, you are interested in what you want. You are eternally interested in it. But no one else is. The rest of us are just like you: we are interested in what we want.

So the only way on earth to influence other people is to talk about what they want and show them how to get it.

Remember that tomorrow when you are trying to get somebody to do something. If, for example, you don't want your children to smoke, don't preach at them, and don't talk about what you want; but show them that cigarettes may keep them from making the basketball team or winning the hundred-yard dash.

This is a good thing to remember regardless of whether you are dealing with children or calves or chimpanzees. For example: one day

Ralph Waldo Emerson and his son tried to get a calf into the barn. But they made the common mistake of thinking only of what they wanted: Emerson pushed and his son pulled. But the calf was doing just what they were doing; he was thinking only of what he wanted, so he stiffened his legs and stubbornly refused to leave the pasture. The Irish housemaid saw their predicament. She couldn't write essays and books; but, on this occasion at least, she had more horse sense, or calf sense, than Emerson had. She thought of what the calf wanted, so she put her maternal finger in the calf's mouth and let the calf suck her finger as she gently led him into the barn.

Every act you have ever performed since the day you were born was performed because you wanted something. How about the time you gave a large contribution to the Red Cross? Yes, that is no exception to the rule. You gave the Red Cross the donation because you wanted to lend a helping hand; you wanted to do a beautiful, unselfish, divine act. "Inasmuch as ye have done it unto one of the least of these my brethren, ye have done it unto me."

If you hadn't wanted that feeling more than you wanted your money, you would not have made the contribution. Of course, you might have made the contribution because you were ashamed to refuse or because a customer asked you to do it. But one thing is certain. You made the contribution because you wanted something.

Harry A. Overstreet in his illuminating book *Influencing Human Behavior* said, "Action springs out of what we fundamentally desire, and the best piece of advice which can be given to would-be persuaders, whether in business, in the home, in the school, in politics, is: First, arouse in the other person an eager want. He who can do this has the whole world with him. He who cannot walk a lonely way."

Andrew Carnegie, the poverty-stricken Scotch lad who started to work at two cents an hour and finally gave away $365 million, learned early in life that the only way to influence people is to talk in terms of what the other person wants. He attended school only four years; yet he learned how to handle people.

To illustrate: His sister-in-law was worried sick over her two boys. They were at Yale, and they were so busy with their own affairs that they neglected to write home and paid no attention whatsoever to their mother's frantic letters.

Then Carnegie offered to wager a hundred dollars that he could get an answer by return mail, without even asking for it. Someone called his bet, so he wrote his nephews a chatty letter, mentioning casually in a postscript that he was sending each one a five-dollar bill.

He neglected, however, to enclose the money.

Back came replies by return mail thanking "Dear Uncle Andrew" for his kind note and...you can finish the sentence yourself.

Another example of persuading comes from Stan Novak of Cleveland, Ohio, a participant in our course. Stan came home from work one evening to find his youngest son, Tim, kicking and screaming on the living room floor. He was to start kindergarten the next day and was protesting that he would not go. Stan's normal reaction would have been to banish the child to his room and tell him he'd just better make up his mind to go. He had no choice. But tonight, recognizing that this would not really help Tim start kindergarten in the best frame of mind, Stan sat down and thought, "If I were Tim, why would I be excited about going to kindergarten?" He and his wife made a list of all the fun things Tim would do such as finger-painting, singing songs, making new friends. Then they put them into action. "We all started finger-painting on the kitchen table—my wife, Lil, my other son Bob, and myself, all having fun. Soon Tim was peeping around the corner. Next he was begging to participate. 'Oh, no! You have to go to kindergarten first to learn how to finger-paint.' With all the enthusiasm I could muster I went through the list talking in terms he could understand, telling him all the fun he would have in kindergarten. The next morning, I thought I was the first one up. I went downstairs and found Tim sitting sound asleep in the living room chair. 'What are you doing here?' I asked. 'I'm waiting to go to kindergarten. I don't want to be late.' The enthusiasm of our entire family had aroused in Tim an eager want that no amount of discussion or threat could have possibly accomplished."

Tomorrow you may want to persuade somebody to do something. Before you speak, pause and ask yourself: "How can I make this person want to do it?"

That question will stop us from rushing into a situation heedlessly, with futile chatter about our desires.

At one time I rented the grand ballroom of a certain New York hotel for twenty nights in each season in order to hold a series of lectures.

At the beginning of one season, I was suddenly informed that I should have to pay almost three times as much rent as formerly.

This news reached me after the tickets had been printed and distributed and all announcements had been made.

Naturally, I didn't want to pay the increase, but what was the use of talking to the hotel about what I wanted? They were interested only in what they wanted. So a couple of days later I went to see the manager.

"I was a bit shocked when I got your letter," I said, "but I don't blame you at all. If I had been in your position, I should probably have written a similar letter myself. Your duty as the manager of the hotel is to make all the profit possible. If you don't do that, you will be fired and you ought to be fired. Now, let's take a piece of paper and write down the advantages and the disadvantages that will accrue to you, if you insist on this increase in rent."

Then I took a letterhead and ran a line through the center and headed one column 'Advantages' and the other column 'Disadvantages'.

I wrote down under the head 'Advantages' these words: "Ballroom free". Then I went on to say, "You will have the advantage of having the ballroom free to rent for dances and conventions. That is a big advantage, for affairs like that will pay you much more than you can get for a series of lectures. If I tie your ballroom up for twenty nights during the course of the season, it is sure to mean a loss of some very profitable business to you.

"Now, let's consider the disadvantages. First, instead of increasing your income from me, you are going to decrease it. In fact, you are going to wipe it out because I cannot pay the rent you are asking for. I shall be forced to hold these lectures at some other place.

"There's another disadvantage to you also. These lectures attract crowds of educated and cultured people to your hotel. That is good advertising for you, isn't it? In fact, if you spent five thousand dollars advertising in the newspapers, you couldn't bring as many people to look at your hotel as I can bring by these lectures. That is worth a lot to a hotel, isn't it?"

As I talked, I wrote these two 'disadvantages' under the proper heading, and handed the sheet of paper to the manager, saying, "I wish you would carefully consider both the advantages and disadvantages that are going to accrue to you and then give me your final decision."

I received a letter the next day, informing me that my rent would be increased only 50 percent instead of 300 percent.

Mind you, I got this reduction without saying a word about what I wanted. I talked all the time about what the other person wanted and how he could get it.

Suppose I had done the human, natural thing; suppose I had stormed into his office and said, "What do you mean by raising my rent three hundred percent when you know the tickets have been printed and the announcements made? Three hundred percent! Ridiculous! Absurd! I won't pay for it!"

What would have happened then? An argument would have begun to steam and boil and sputter, and you know how arguments end. Even if I had convinced him that he was wrong, his pride would have made it difficult for him to back down and give in.

Here is one of the best bits of advice ever given about the fine art of human relationships. "If there is any one secret of success," said Henry Ford, "it lies in the ability to get the other person's point of view and see things from that person's angle as well as from your own."

That is so good, I want to repeat it: "If there is any one secret of success, it lies in the ability to get the other person's point of view and see things from that person's angle as well as from your own."

That is so simple, so obvious, that anyone ought to see the truth of it at a glance; yet 90 percent of the people on this earth ignore it 90 percent of the time.

An example? Look at the letters that come across your desk tomorrow morning, and you will find that most of them violate this important canon of common sense. Take this one, a letter written by the head of the radio department of an advertising agency with offices scattered across the continent. This letter was sent to the managers of local radio stations throughout the country (I have set down, in brackets, my reactions to each paragraph).

Mr. John Blank,
Blankville,
Indiana

Dear Mr. Blank,

The ------ company desires to retain its position in advertising agency leadership in the radio field.
[Who cares what your company desires? I am worried about my own problems. The bank is foreclosing the mortgage on my house, the bugs are destroying the hollyhocks, the stock market tumbled yesterday. I missed the eight-fifteen this morning, I wasn't invited to Jones's dance last night, the doctor tells me I have high blood pressure and neuritis and dandruff. And then what happens? I came down to the office this morning worried, opened my mail and here is some little whippersnapper off in New York yapping about what his company wants. Bah! If he only realized what sort of impression his letter makes, he would get out of the advertising business and start manufacturing sheep dip.]

This agency's national advertising accounts were the bulwark of the network. Our subsequent clearances of station time have kept us at the top of agencies year after year.

[You are big and rich and right at the top, are you? So what? I don't give two whoops in Hades if you are as big as General Motors and General Electric and the General Staff of the U.S. Army all combined. If you had as much sense as a half-witted hummingbird, you would realize that I am interested in how big I am, not how big you are. All this talk about your enormous success makes me feel small and unimportant.]

We desire to service our accounts with the last word on radio station information.

[You desire! You desire. You unmitigated ass. I'm not interested in what you desire or what the President of the United States desires. Let me tell you once and for all that I am interested in what I desire, and you haven't said a word about that yet in this absurd letter of yours.]

Will you, therefore, put the ------ company on your preferred list for weekly station information every single detail that will be useful to an agency in intelligently booking time.

[Preferred list! You have your nerve! You make me feel insignificant by your big talk about your company and then you ask me to put you on a 'preferred' list, and you don't even say 'please' when you ask it.]

A prompt acknowledgment of this letter, giving us your latest 'doings', will be mutually helpful.

[You fool! You mail me a cheap form letter—a letter scattered far and wide like the autumn leaves—and you have the gall to ask me, when I am worried about the mortgage and the hollyhocks and my blood pressure, to sit down and dictate a personal note acknowledging your form letter, and you ask me to do it 'promptly'. What do you mean, 'promptly'? Don't you know I am just as busy as you are—or, at least, I like to think I am. And while we are on the subject, who gave you the lordly right to order me around? You say it will be 'mutually helpful'. At last, at last, you have begun to see my viewpoint. But you are vague about how it will be to my advantage.]

Very truly yours,
John Doe
Manager Radio Department

P.S. The enclosed reprint from the Blankville Journal will be of interest to you, and you may want to broadcast it over your station.

[Finally, down here in the postscript, you mention something that may help me solve one of my problems. Why didn't you begin your letter with, but what's the use? Any advertising man who is guilty of perpetrating such drivel as you have sent me has something wrong with his medulla oblongata. You don't need a letter giving our latest doings. What you need is a quart of iodine in your thyroid gland.]

Now, if people who devote their lives to advertising and who pose as experts in the art of influencing people to buy, if they write a letter like that, what can we expect from the butcher and baker or the auto mechanic?

Here is another letter, written by the superintendent of a large freight terminal to a student of this course, Edward Vermylen. What effect did this letter have on the man to whom it was addressed? Read it and then I'll tell you.

A. Zerega's Sons, Inc.
28 Front St. Brooklyn, N.Y. 11201
Attention: Mr. Edward Vermylen

Gentlemen,

The operations at our outbound-rail-receiving station are handicapped because a material percentage of the total business is delivered to us in the late afternoon. This condition results in congestion, overtime on the part of our forces, delays to trucks, and in some cases delays to freight. On November 10, we received from your company a lot of 510 pieces, which reached here at 4:20 P.M.

We solicit your cooperation toward overcoming the undesirable effects arising from late receipt of freight. May we ask that, on days on which you ship the volume which was received on the above date, effort be made either to get the truck here earlier or to deliver us part of the freight during the morning?

The advantage that would accrue to you under such an arrangement would be that of more expeditious discharge of your trucks and the assurance that your business would go forward on the date of its receipt.

Very truly yours,

J----- B----- Supt.

After reading this letter, Mr. Vermylen, sales manager for A. Zerega's Sons, Inc., sent it to me with the following comment:

This letter had the reverse effect from that which was intended. The letter begins by describing the Terminal's difficulties, in which we are not interested, generally speaking. Our cooperation is then requested without any thought as to whether it would inconvenience us, and then, finally, in the last paragraph, the fact is mentioned that if we do cooperate it will mean more expeditious discharge of our trucks with the assurance that our freight will go forward on the date of its receipt. In other words, that in which we are most interested is mentioned last and the whole effect is one of raising a spirit of antagonism rather than of cooperation.

Let's see if we can't rewrite and improve this letter. Let's not waste any time talking about our problems. As Henry Ford admonishes, let's "get the other person's point of view and see things from his or her angle, as well as from our own."

Here is one way of revising the letter. It may not be the best way, but isn't it an improvement?

Mr. Edward Vermylen
A. Zerega's Sons, Inc.
28 Front St.
Brooklyn, N.Y. 11201

Dear Mr. Vermylen,

Your company has been one of our good customers for fourteen years. Naturally, we are very grateful for your patronage and are eager to give you the speedy, efficient service you deserve. However, we regret to say that it isn't possible for us to do that when your trucks bring us a large shipment late in the afternoon, as they did on November 10. Why? Because many other customers make late afternoon deliveries also. Naturally, that causes congestion. That means your trucks are held up unavoidably at the pier and sometimes even your freight is delayed.

That's bad, but it can be avoided. If you make your deliveries at the pier in the morning when possible, your trucks will be able to keep moving, your freight will get immediate attention, and our workers will get home early at night to enjoy a dinner of the delicious macaroni and noodles that you manufacture.

Regardless of when your shipments arrive, we shall always cheerfully do all in our power to serve you promptly. You are busy. Please don't trouble to answer this note.

Yours truly,
J----- B-----, supt.

Barbara Anderson, who worked in a bank in New York, desired to move to Phoenix, Arizona, because of the health of her son. Using the principles she had learned in our course, she wrote the following letter to twelve banks in Phoenix:

Dear Sir,

My ten years of bank experience should be of interest to a rapidly growing bank like yours.

In various capacities in bank operations with the Bankers Trust Company in New York, leading to my present assignment as Branch Manager, I have acquired skills in all phases of banking including depositor relations, credits, loans, and administration.

I will be relocating to Phoenix in May and I am sure I can contribute to your growth and profit. I will be in Phoenix the week of April 3 and would appreciate the opportunity to show you how I can help your bank meet its goals.

Sincerely,
Barbara L. Anderson

Do you think Mrs. Anderson received any response from that letter? Eleven of the twelve banks invited her to be interviewed, and she had a choice of which bank's offer to accept. Why? Mrs. Anderson did not state what she wanted, but wrote in the letter how she could help them, and focused on their wants, not her own.

Thousands of salespeople are pounding the pavements today, tired, discouraged, and underpaid. Why? Because they are always thinking only of what they want. They don't realize that neither you nor I want to buy anything. If we did, we would go out and buy it. But both of us are eternally interested in solving our problems. And if salespeople can show us how their services or merchandise will help us solve our problems, they won't need to sell us. We'll buy it. And customers like to feel that they are buying, not being sold.

Yet many salespeople spend a lifetime selling without seeing things from the customer's angle. For example, for many years I lived in Forest Hills, a little community of private homes in the center of Greater New York. One day as I was rushing to the station, I chanced to meet a real-estate operator who had bought and sold property in that area for many years. He knew Forest Hills well, so I hurriedly asked him whether or not my stucco house was built with metal lath or hollow tile. He said he didn't know and told me what I already knew, that I could find out by calling the Forest Hills Garden Association. The following morning, I received a letter from him. Did he give me the information I wanted? He could have gotten it in sixty seconds by a telephone call. But he didn't. He told me again that I could get it by telephoning, and then asked me to let him handle my insurance.

He was not interested in helping me. He was interested only in helping himself.

J. Howard Lucas of Birmingham, Alabama, tells how two salespeople from the same company handled the same type of situation. He reported:

"Several years ago I was on the management team of a small company. Headquartered near us was the district office of a large insurance company. Their agents were assigned territories, and our company was assigned to two agents, whom I shall refer to as Carl and John.

"One morning, Carl dropped by our office and casually mentioned that his company had just introduced a new life insurance policy for executives and thought we might be interested later on and he would get back to us when he had more information on it.

"The same day, John saw us on the sidewalk while returning from a coffee break, and he shouted, 'Hey Luke, hold up, I have some great news for you fellows.' He hurried over and very excitedly told us about an executive life insurance policy his company had introduced that very day (it was the same policy that Carl had casually mentioned). He wanted us to have one of the first issues. He gave us a few important facts about the coverage and ended saying, 'The policy is so new, I'm going to have someone from the home office come out tomorrow and explain it. Now, in the meantime, let's get the applications signed and on the way so he can have more information to work with.' His enthusiasm aroused in us an eager want for this policy even though we still did not have details. When they were made available to us, they confirmed John's initial understanding of the policy, and he not only sold each of us a policy, but later doubled our coverage.

"Carl could have had those sales, but he made no effort to arouse in us any desire for the policies."

The world is full of people who are grabbing and self-seeking. So the rare individual who unselfishly tries to serve others has an enormous advantage. He has little competition. Owen D. Young, a noted lawyer and one of America's great business leaders, once said, "People who can put themselves in the place of other people who can understand the workings of their minds, need never worry about what the future has in store for them."

If out of reading this book you get just one thing—an increased tendency to think always in terms of other people's point of view, and see things from their angle—if you get that one thing out of this book, it may easily prove to be one of the building blocks of your career.

Looking at the other person's point of view and arousing in him an eager want for something is not to be construed as manipulating that person so that he will do something that is only for your benefit and his detriment. Each party should gain from the negotiation. In the letters to Mr. Vermylen, both the sender and the receiver of the correspondence gained by implementing what was suggested. Both the bank and Mrs. Anderson won by her letter in that the bank obtained a valuable employee and Mrs. Anderson a suitable job. And in the example of John's sale of insurance to Mr. Lucas, both gained through this transaction.

Another example in which everybody gains through this principle of arousing an eager want comes from Michael E. Whidden of Warwick, Rhode Island, who is a territory salesman for the Shell Oil Company. Mike wanted to become the Number One salesperson in his district, but one service station was holding him back. It was run by an older man who could not be motivated to clean up his station. It was in such poor shape that sales were declining significantly.

This manager would not listen to any of Mike's pleas to upgrade the station. After many exhortations and heart-to-heart talks—all of which had no impact—Mike decided to invite the manager to visit the newest Shell station in his territory.

The manager was so impressed by the facilities at the new station that when Mike visited him the next time, his station was cleaned up and had recorded a sales increase. This enabled Mike to reach the Number One spot in his district. All his talking and discussion hadn't helped, but by arousing an eager want in the manager, by showing him the modern station, he had accomplished his goal, and both the manager and Mike benefited.

Most people go through college and learn to read Virgil and master the mysteries of calculus without ever discovering how their own minds function. For instance: I once gave a course in Effective Speaking for the young college graduates who were entering the employ of the Carrier Corporation, the large air-conditioner manufacturer. One of the participants wanted to persuade the others to play basketball in their free time, and this is about what he said, "I want you to come out and play basketball. I like to play basketball, but the last few times I've been to the gymnasium there haven't been enough people to get up a game. Two or three of us got to throw the ball around the other night—and I got a black eye. I wish all of you would come down tomorrow night. I want to play basketball."

Did he talk about anything you want? You don't want to go to a gymnasium that no one else goes to, do you? You don't care about what he wants. You don't want to get a black eye.

Could he have shown you how to get the things you want by using the gymnasium? Surely. More pep. Keener edge to the appetite. Clearer brain. Fun. Games. Basketball.

To repeat Professor Overstreet's wise advice: First, arouse in the other person an eager want. He who can do this has the whole world with him. He who cannot walk a lonely way.

One of the students in the author's training course was worried about his little boy. The child was underweight and refused to eat properly. His parents used the usual method. They scolded and nagged. "Mother wants you to eat this and that." "Father wants you to grow up to be a big man."

Did the boy pay any attention to these pleas? Just about as much as you pay for one fleck of sand on a sandy beach.

No one with a trace of horse sense would expect a child three years old to react to the viewpoint of a father thirty years old. Yet that was precisely what that father had expected. It was absurd. He finally saw that.

So he said to himself, "What does that boy want? How can I tie up what I want to what he wants?"

It was easy for the father when he started thinking about it. His boy had a tricycle that he loved to ride up and down the sidewalk in front of the house in Brooklyn. A few doors down the street lived a bully—a bigger boy who would pull the little boy off his tricycle and ride it himself.

Naturally, the little boy would run screaming to his mother, and she would have to come out and take the bully off the tricycle and put her little boy on again. This happens almost every day.

What did the little boy want? It didn't take Sherlock Holmes to answer that one. His pride, his anger, his desire for a feeling of importance—all the strongest emotions in his makeup—goaded him to get revenge, to smash the bully in the nose. And when his father explained that the boy would be able to wallop the daylights out of the bigger kid someday if he would only eat the things his mother wanted him to eat—when his father promised him that—there was no longer any problem with dietetics. That boy would have eaten spinach, sauerkraut, salt mackerel—anything in order to be big enough to whip the bully who had humiliated him so often.

After solving that problem, the parents tackled another: the little boy had the unholy habit of wetting his bed.

He slept with his grandmother. In the morning, his grandmother would wake up and feel the sheet and say, "Look, Johnny, what you did again last night."

He would say, "No, I didn't do it. You did it."

Scolding, spanking, shaming him, reiterating that the parents didn't want him to do it—none of these things kept the bed dry. So the parents asked, "How can we make this boy want to stop wetting his bed?"

What were his wants? First, he wanted to wear pajamas like Daddy instead of wearing a nightgown like Grandmother. Grandmother was getting fed up with his nocturnal iniquities, so she gladly offered to buy him a pair of pajamas if he would reform. Second, he wanted a bed of his own. Grandma didn't object.

His mother took him to a department store in Brooklyn, winked at the salesgirl, and said, "Here is a little gentleman who would like to do some shopping."

The salesgirl made him feel important by saying, "Young man, what can I show you?"

He stood a couple of inches taller and said, "I want to buy a bed for myself."

When he was shown the one his mother wanted him to buy, she winked at the salesgirl and the boy was persuaded to buy it.

The bed was delivered the next day; and that night, when Father came home, the little boy ran to the door shouting, "Daddy! Daddy! Come upstairs and see the bed that I bought!"

The father, looking at the bed, obeyed Charles Schwab's injunction: he was "hearty in his approbation and lavish in his praise."

"You are not going to wet this bed, are you?" the father said. "Oh, no, no! I am not going to wet this bed." The boy kept his promise, for his pride was involved. That was his bed. He and he alone had bought it. And he was wearing pajamas now like a little man. He wanted to act like a man. And he did.

Another father, K. T. Dutschmann, a telephone engineer, a student of this course, couldn't get his three-year-old daughter to eat breakfast food. The usual scolding, pleading, coaxing methods had all ended in futility.

So the parents asked themselves, "How can we make her want to do it?"

The little girl loved to imitate her mother, to feel big and grown up; so one morning they put her on a chair and let her make the breakfast food. At just the psychological moment, Father drifted into the kitchen while she was stirring the cereal and she said, "Oh, look, Daddy, I am making the cereal this morning."

She ate two helpings of the cereal without any coaxing, because she was interested in it. She had achieved a feeling of importance; she had found in making the cereal an avenue of self-expression.

William Winter once remarked that "self-expression is the dominant necessity of human nature." Why can't we adapt this same psychology to business dealings? When we have a brilliant idea, instead of making others think it is ours, why not let them cook and stir the idea themselves? They will then regard it as their own; they will like it and maybe eat a couple of helpings of it.

Remember: "First, arouse in the other person an eager want. He who can do this has the whole world with him. He who cannot walk a lonely way."

⇒ PRINCIPLE 3 ⇐

Arouse in the other person an eager want.

→ In a Nutshell ←

FUNDAMENTAL TECHNIQUES IN HANDLING PEOPLE

⇒ PRINCIPLE 1 ⇐

Don't criticize, condemn, or complain.

⇒ PRINCIPLE 2 ⇐

Give honest and sincere appreciation.

⇒ PRINCIPLE 3 ⇐

Arouse in the other person an eager want.

PART TWO

Six Ways To Make People Like You

↣ 4 ↢

"DO THIS AND YOU'LL BE WELCOME ANYWHERE."

Why read this book to find out how to win friends? Why not study the technique of the greatest winner of friends the world has ever known? Who is he? You may meet him tomorrow coming down the street. When you get within ten feet of him, he will begin to wag his tail. If you stop and pat him, he will almost jump out of his skin to show you how much he likes you. And you know that behind this show of affection on his part, there are no ulterior motives: he doesn't want to sell you any real estate, and he doesn't want to marry you.

Did you ever stop to think that a dog is the only animal that doesn't have to work for a living? A hen has to lay eggs, a cow has to give milk, and a canary has to sing. But a dog makes his living by giving you nothing but love.

When I was five years old, my father bought a little yellow-haired pup for fifty cents. He was the light and joy of my childhood. Every afternoon about four-thirty, he would sit in the front yard with his beautiful eyes staring steadfastly at the path, and as soon as he heard my voice or saw me swinging my dinner pail through the buck brush, he was off like a shot, racing breathlessly up the hill to greet me with leaps of joy and barks of sheer ecstasy.

Tippy was my constant companion for five years. Then one tragic night—I shall never forget it—he was killed within ten feet of my head, killed by lightning. Tippy's death was the tragedy of my boyhood.

You never read a book on psychology, Tippy. You didn't need to. You knew by some divine instinct that you can make more friends in two months by becoming genuinely interested in other people than you can in two years by trying to get other people interested in you. Let me repeat that. You can make more friends in two months by becoming interested in other people than you can in two years by trying to get other people interested in you.

Yet I know and you know people who blunder through life trying to wigwag other people into becoming interested in them.

Of course, it doesn't work. People are not interested in you. They are not interested in me. They are interested in themselves—morning, noon, and after dinner.

The New York Telephone Company made a detailed study of telephone conversations to find out which word is the most frequently used. You have guessed it: it is the personal pronoun "I." "I." "I." It was used 3,900 times in 500 telephone conversations. "I." "I." "I." "I." When you see a group photograph that you are in, whose picture do you look for first?

If we merely try to impress people and get people interested in us, we will never have many true, sincere friends. Friends, real friends, are not made that way.

Napoleon tried it, and in his last meeting with Josephine he said, "Josephine, I have been as fortunate as any man ever was on this earth; and yet, at this hour, you are the only person in the world on whom I can rely." And historians doubt whether he could rely even on her.

Alfred Adler, the famous Viennese psychologist, wrote a book entitled *What Life Should Mean to You*. In that book he says, "It is the individual who is not interested in his fellow men who has the greatest difficulties in life and provides the greatest injury to others. It is from among such individuals that all human failures spring."

You may read scores of erudite tomes on psychology without coming across a statement more significant for you and for me. Adler's statement is so rich with meaning that I am going to repeat it in italics: *It is the individual who is not interested in his fellow men who has the greatest difficulties in life and provides the greatest injury to others. It is from among such individuals that all human failures spring.*

I once took a course in short-story writing at New York University, and during that course the editor of a leading magazine talked to our class. He said he could pick up any one of the dozens of stories that drifted across his desk every day and after reading a few paragraphs he could feel whether or not the author liked people. "If the author doesn't like people," he said, "people won't like his or her stories."

This hard-boiled editor stopped twice in the course of his talk on fiction writing and apologized for preaching a sermon. "I am telling you," he said, "the same things your preacher would tell you, but remember, you have to be interested in people if you want to be a successful writer of stories."

If that is true of writing fiction, you can be sure it is true of dealing with people face-to-face.

I spent an evening in the dressing room of Howard Thurston the last time he appeared on Broadway. Thurston was the acknowledged dean of magicians. For forty years he had traveled all over the world, time and again, creating illusions, mystifying audiences, and making people gasp with astonishment. More than 60 million people had paid admission to his show, and he had made almost $2 million in profit.

I asked Mr. Thurston to tell me the secret of his success. His schooling certainly had nothing to do with it, for he ran away from home as a small boy, became a hobo, rode in boxcars, slept in haystacks, begged his food from door to door, and learned to read by looking out of boxcars at signs along the railway.

Did he have a superior knowledge of magic? No, he told me hundreds of books had been written about legerdemain and scores of people knew as much about it as he did. But he had two things that the others didn't have. First, he had the ability to put his personality across the footlights. He was a master showman. He knew human nature. Everything he did, every gesture, every intonation of his voice, every lifting of an eyebrow had been carefully rehearsed in advance, and his actions were timed to split seconds. But, in addition to that, Thurston had a genuine interest in people. He told me that many magicians would look at the audience and say to themselves, "Well, there are a bunch of suckers out there, a bunch of hicks; I'll fool them all right." But Thurston's method was totally different. He told me that every time he went on stage he said to himself, "I am grateful because these people come to see me. They make it possible for me to make my living in a very agreeable way. I'm going to give them the very best I possibly can."

He declared he never stepped in front of the footlights without first saying to himself over and over, "I love my audience. I love my audience." Ridiculous? Absurd? You are privileged to think anything you like. I am merely passing it on to you without comment as a recipe used by one of the most famous magicians of all time.

George Dyke of North Warren, Pennsylvania, was forced to retire from his service station business after thirty years when a new highway was constructed over the site of his station. It wasn't long before the idle days of retirement began to bore him, so he started filling in his time trying to play music on his old fiddle. Soon he was traveling the area to listen to music and talk with many of the accomplished fiddlers. In his humble and friendly way he became generally interested in learning the background and interests of every musician he met. Although he was not a great fiddler himself, he made many friends in this pursuit. He attended competitions and soon became known to the country music fans in the eastern part of the United States as "Uncle George, the Fiddle Scraper from Kinzua County." When we heard Uncle George, he was seventy-two and enjoying every minute of his life. By having a sustained interest in other people, he created a new life for himself at a time when most people consider their productive years over.

That, too, was one of the secrets of Theodore Roosevelt's astonishing popularity. Even his servants loved him. His valet, James E. Amos, wrote a book about him entitled *Theodore Roosevelt, Hero to His Valet*.

In that book Amos relates this illuminating incident: "My wife one time asked the President about a bobwhite. She had never seen one and he described it to her fully. Sometime later, the telephone at our cottage rang. [Amos and his wife lived in a little cottage on the Roosevelt estate at Oyster Bay.] My wife answered it and it was Mr. Roosevelt himself. He had called her, he said, to tell her that there was a bobwhite outside her window and that if she would look out she might see it. Little things like that were so characteristic of him. Whenever he went by our cottage, even though we were out of sight, we would hear him call out, 'Oo-oo-oo, Annie?' or 'Oo-oo-oo, James!' It was just a friendly greeting as he went by."

How could employees keep from liking a man like that? How could anyone keep from liking him? Roosevelt called at the White House one day when the President and Mrs. Taft were away. His honest liking for humble people was shown by the fact that he greeted all the old White House servants by name, even the scullery maids.

"When he saw Alice, the kitchen maid," writes Archie Butt, "he asked her if she still made corn bread. Alice told him that she sometimes made it for the servants, but no one ate it upstairs.

"'They show bad taste,' Roosevelt boomed, 'and I'll tell the President when I see him.'

"Alice brought a piece to him on a plate, and he went over to the office eating it as he went and greeting gardeners and laborers as he passed...

"He addressed each person just as he had addressed them in the past. Ike Hoover, who had been head usher at the White House for forty years, said with tears in his eyes, 'It is the only happy day we had in nearly two years, and not one of us would exchange it for a hundred-dollar bill.'"

The same concern for the seemingly unimportant people helped sales representative Edward M. Sykes, Jr., of Chatham, New Jersey, retain an account. "Many years ago," he reported, "I called on customers for Johnson & Johnson in the Massachusetts area. One account was a drugstore in Hingham. Whenever I went into this store I would always talk to the soda clerk and sales clerk for a few minutes before talking to the owner to obtain his order. One day I went up to the owner of the store, and he told me to leave as he was not interested in buying J&J products anymore because he felt they were concentrating their activities on food and discount stores to the detriment of the small drugstore. I left with my tail between my legs and drove around the town for several hours. Finally, I decided to go back and try at least to explain our position to the owner of the store.

"When I returned I walked in and as usual said hello to the soda clerk and sales clerk. When I walked up to the owner, he smiled at me and welcomed me back. He then gave me double the usual order. I looked at him with surprise and asked him what had happened since my visit only a few hours earlier. He pointed to the young man at the soda fountain and said that after I had left, the boy had come over and said that I was one of the few salespeople that called on the store that even bothered to say hello to him and to the others in the store. He told the owner that if any salesperson deserved his business, it was I. The owner agreed and remained a loyal customer. I never forgot that to be genuinely interested in other people is a most important quality for a salesperson to possess—for any person, for that matter."

I have discovered from personal experience that one can win the attention and time and cooperation of even the most sought-after people by becoming genuinely interested in them. Let me illustrate.

Years ago I conducted a course in fiction writing at the Brooklyn Institute of Arts and Sciences, and we wanted such distinguished and busy authors as Kathleen Norris, Fannie Hurst, Ida Tarbell, Albert Payson Terhune, and Rupert Hughes to come to Brooklyn and give us the benefit of their experiences. So we wrote to them, saying we admired their work and were deeply interested in getting their advice and learning the secrets of their success.

Each of these letters was signed by about a hundred and fifty students. We said we realized that these authors were busy—too busy to prepare a lecture. So we enclosed a list of questions for them to answer about themselves and their methods of work. They liked that. Who wouldn't like it? So they left their homes and traveled to Brooklyn to give us a helping hand.

By using the same method, I persuaded Leslie M. Shaw, secretary of the treasury in Theodore Roosevelt's cabinet; George W. Wickersham, attorney general in Taft's cabinet; William Jennings Bryan; Franklin D.

Roosevelt, and many other prominent men to come to talk to the students of my courses in public speaking.

All of us, be we workers in a factory, clerks in an office, or even a king upon his throne—all of us like people who admire us. Take the German Kaiser, for example. At the close of World War I he was probably the most savagely and universally despised man on this earth. Even his own nation turned against him when he fled over into Holland to save his neck. The hatred against him was so intense that millions of people would have loved to tear him limb from limb or burn him at the stake. In the midst of all this forest fire of fury, one little boy wrote the Kaiser a simple, sincere letter glowing with kindliness and admiration. This little boy said that no matter what the others thought, he would always love Wilhelm as his Emperor. The Kaiser was deeply touched by his letter and invited the little boy to come to see him. The boy came, so did his mother—and the Kaiser married her. That little boy didn't need to read a book on how to win friends and influence people. He knew how instinctively.

If we want to make friends, let's put ourselves out to do things for other people—things that require time, energy, unselfishness, and thoughtfulness. When the Duke of Windsor was Prince of Wales, he was scheduled to tour South America, and before he started out on that tour he spent months studying Spanish so that he could make public talks in the language of the country; and the South Americans loved him for it.

For years I made it a point to find out the birthdays of my friends. How? Although I haven't the foggiest bit of faith in astrology, I began by asking the other party whether he believed the date of one's birth has anything to do with character and disposition. I then asked him or her to tell me the month and day of birth. If he or she said November 24, for example, I kept repeating to myself, "November 24, November 24." The minute my friend's back was turned, I wrote down the name and birthday and later would transfer it to a birthday book. At the beginning of each year, I had these birthday dates scheduled in my calendar pad so that they came to my attention automatically. When the natal day arrived, there was my letter or telegram. What a hit it made! I was frequently the only person on earth who remembered.

If we want to make friends, let's greet people with animation and enthusiasm. When somebody calls you on the telephone, use the same psychology. Say "Hello" in tones that bespeak how pleased YOU are to have the person call. Many companies train their telephone operators to greet all callers in a tone of voice that radiates interest and enthusiasm. The caller feels the company is concerned about them. Let's remember that when we answer the telephone tomorrow.

Showing a genuine interest in others not only wins friends for you, but may develop in its customers a loyalty to your company. In an issue of the publication of the National Bank of North America of New York, the following letter from Madeline Rosedale, a depositor, was published*:

* *Eagle*, publication of the National Bank of North America, New York, March 31, 1978.

"I would like you to know how much I appreciate your staff. Everyone is so courteous, polite, and helpful. What a pleasure it is, after waiting in a long line, to have the teller greet you pleasantly.

"Last year my mother was hospitalized for five months. Frequently I went to Marie Petrucello, a teller. She was concerned about my mother and inquired about her progress."

Is there any doubt that Mrs. Rosedale will continue to use this bank?

Charles R. Walters, of one of the large banks in New York City, was assigned to prepare a confidential report on a certain corporation. He knew of only one person who possessed the facts he needed so urgently. As Mr. Walters was ushered into the president's office, a young woman stuck her head through a door and told the president that she didn't have any stamps for him that day.

"I am collecting stamps for my twelve-year-old son," the president explained to Mr. Walters.

Mr. Walters stated his mission and began asking questions. The president was vague, general, nebulous. He didn't want to talk, and apparently nothing could persuade him to talk. The interview was brief and barren.

"Frankly, I didn't know what to do," Mr. Walters said as he related the story to the class. "Then I remembered what his secretary had said to him—stamps, twelve-year-old son...and I also recalled that the foreign department of our bank collected stamps—stamps taken from letters pouring in from every continent washed by the seven seas.

"The next afternoon I called on this man and sent in word that I had some stamps for his boy. Was I ushered in with enthusiasm? Yes, sir! He couldn't have shaken my hand with more enthusiasm if he had been running for Congress. He radiated smiles and goodwill. 'My George will love this one,' he kept saying as he fondled the stamps. 'And look at this! This is a treasure.'

"We spent half an hour talking stamps and looking at a picture of his boy, and he then devoted more than an hour of his time to giving me every bit of information I wanted—without even suggesting that he do it. He told me all he knew, and then called in his subordinates and questioned them. He telephoned some of his associates. He loaded me down with facts, figures, reports, and correspondence. In the parlance of newspaper reporters, I had a scoop."

Here is another illustration: C. M. Knaphle, Jr., of Philadelphia had tried for years to sell fuel to a large chain-store organization. But the chain-store company continued to purchase its fuel from an out-of-town dealer and haul it right past the door of Knaphle's office. Mr. Knaphle made a speech one night before one of my classes, pouring out his hot wrath upon chain stores, branding them as a curse to the nation.

And still he wondered why he couldn't sell them.

I suggested that he try different tactics. To put it briefly, this is what happened. We staged a debate between members of the course on whether the spread of the chain store is doing the country more harm than good.

Knaphle, at my suggestion, took the negative side; he agreed to defend the chain stores, and then went straight to an executive of the chain-store organization that he despised and said, "I am not here to try to sell fuel. I have come to ask you to do me a favor." He then talked about his debate and said, "I have come to you for help because I can't think of anyone else who would be more capable of giving me the facts I want. I'm anxious to win this debate, and I'll deeply appreciate whatever help you can give me."

Here is the rest of the story in Mr. Knaphle's own words: "I had asked this man for precisely one minute of his time. It was with that understanding that he consented to see me. After I had stated my case, he motioned me to a chair and talked to me for exactly one hour and forty-seven minutes. He called in another executive who had written a book on chain stores. He wrote to the National Chain Store Association and secured for me a copy of a debate on the subject. He feels that the chain store is rendering a real service to humanity. He is proud of what he is doing for hundreds of communities. His eyes fairly glowed as he talked, and I must confess that he opened my eyes to things I had never even dreamed of. He changed my whole mental attitude. As I was leaving, he walked with me to the door, put his arm around my shoulder, wished me well in my debate, and asked me to stop in and see him again and let him know how I made out. The last words he said to me were: 'Please see me again later in the spring. I should like to place an order with you for fuel.'"

To me that was almost a miracle. Here he was offering to buy fuel without my even suggesting it. I had made more headway in two hours by becoming genuinely interested in him and his problems than I could have made in ten years trying to get him interested in me and my product.

You didn't discover a new truth, Mr. Knaphle, for, a long time ago, a hundred years before Christ was born a famous old Roman poet, Publilius Syrus, remarked, "We are interested in others when they are interested in us."

A show of interest, as with every other principle of human relations, must be sincere. It must pay off not only for the person showing the interest, but for the person receiving the attention. It is a two-way street—both parties benefit.

Martin Ginsberg, who took our Course in Long Island, New York, reported how the special interest a nurse took in him profoundly affected his life:

"It was Thanksgiving Day and I was ten years old. I was in a welfare ward of a city hospital and was scheduled to undergo major orthopedic surgery the next day. I knew that I could only look forward to months of confinement, convalescence, and pain. My father was dead; my mother and I lived alone in a small apartment and we were on welfare. My mother was unable to visit me that day.

"As the day went on, I became overwhelmed with the feeling of loneliness, despair, and fear. I knew my mother was home alone worrying about me, not having anyone to be with, not having anyone to eat with, and not even having enough money to afford a Thanksgiving Day dinner.

"The tears welled up in my eyes, and I stuck my head under the pillow and pulled the covers over it. I cried silently, but oh so bitterly, so much that my body racked with pain.

"A young student nurse heard my sobbing and came over to me. She took the covers off my face and started wiping my tears. She told me how lonely she was, having to work that day and not being able to be with her family. She asked me whether I would have dinner with her. She brought two trays of food: sliced turkey, mashed potatoes, cranberry sauce, and ice cream for dessert. She talked to me, and tried to calm my fears. Even though she was scheduled to go off duty at 4 P.M., she stayed on her own time until almost 11 P.M. She played games with me, talked to me, and stayed with me until I finally fell asleep.

"Many Thanksgivings have come and gone since I was ten, but one never passes without me remembering that particular one and my feelings of frustration, fear, loneliness, and the warmth and tenderness of the stranger that somehow made it all bearable."

If you want others to like you, if you want to develop real friendships, if you want to help others at the same time as you help yourself, keep this principle in mind:

⇒ PRINCIPLE 1 ⇐

Become genuinely interested in other people.

↣ 5 ↢

"A SIMPLE WAY TO MAKE A GOOD IMPRESSION."

At a dinner party in New York, one of the guests, a woman who had inherited money, was eager to make a pleasing impression on everyone. She had squandered a modest fortune on sables, diamonds and pearls. But she hadn't done anything about her face. It radiated sourness and selfishness. She didn't realize what everyone knows: namely, that the expression one wears on one's face is far more important than the clothes one wears on one's back.

Charles Schwab told me his smile had been worth a million dollars. And he was probably understating the truth. Schwab's personality, his charm, his ability to make people like him, were almost wholly responsible for his extraordinary success; and one of the most delightful factors in his personality was his captivating smile.

Actions speak louder than words, and a smile says, "I like you. You make me happy. I am glad to see you." That is why dogs make such a hit. They are so glad to see us that they almost jump out of their skins. So, naturally, we are glad to see them.

A baby's smile has the same effect.

Have you ever been in a doctor's waiting room and looked around at all the glum faces waiting impatiently to be seen? Dr. Stephen K. Sproul, a veterinarian in Raytown, Missouri, told of a typical spring day when his waiting room was full of clients waiting to have their pets inoculated. No one was talking to anyone else, and all were probably thinking of a dozen other things they would rather be doing than "wasting time" sitting in that office. He told one of our classes, "There were six or seven clients waiting when a young woman came in with a nine-month-old baby and a kitten. As luck would have it, she sat down next to a gentleman who was more than a little distraught about the long wait for service. The next thing he knew, the baby just looked up at him with that great big smile that is so characteristic of babies. What did that gentleman do? Just what you and I would do, of course: he smiled back at the baby. Soon he struck up a conversation with the woman about her baby and his grandchildren, and soon the entire reception room joined in, and the boredom and tension were converted into a pleasant and enjoyable experience."

An insincere grin? No. That doesn't fool anybody. We know it is mechanical and we resent it. I am talking about a real smile, a heartwarming smile, a smile that comes from within, the kind of smile that will bring a good price in the marketplace.

Professor James V. McConnell, a psychologist at the University of Michigan, expressed his feelings about a smile. "People who smile," he said, "tend to manage, teach, and sell more effectively, and to raise happier children. There's far more information in a smile than a frown. That's why encouragement is a much more effective teaching device than punishment."

The employment manager of a large New York department store told me she would rather hire a sales clerk who hadn't finished grade school, if he or she has a pleasant smile, than to hire a doctor of philosophy with a somber face.

The effect of a smile is powerful, even when it is unseen. Telephone companies throughout the United States have a program called "phone power" which is offered to employees who use the telephone for selling their services or products. In this program they suggest that you smile when talking on the phone. Your 'smile' comes through in your voice.

Robert Cryer, manager of a computer department for a Cincinnati, Ohio, company, told how he had successfully found the right applicant for a hard-to-fill position, "I was desperately trying to recruit a Ph.D. in computer science for my department. I finally located a young man with ideal qualifications who was about to graduate from Purdue University. After several phone conversations I learned that he had several offers from other companies, many of them larger and better known than mine. I was delighted when he accepted my offer. After he started on the job, I asked him why he had chosen us over the others. He paused for a moment and then he said, 'I think it was because managers in the other companies spoke on the phone in a cold, businesslike manner, which made me feel like just another business transaction. Your voice sounded as if you were glad to hear from me...that you really wanted me to be part of your organization.' You can be assured, I am still answering my phone with a smile."

The chairman of the board of directors of one of the largest rubber companies in the United States told me that, according to his observations, people rarely succeed at anything unless they have fun doing it. This industrial leader doesn't put much faith in the old adage that hard work alone is the magic key that will unlock the door to our desires, "I have known people," he said, "who succeeded because they had a rip-roaring good time conducting their business. Later, I saw those people change as the fun became work. The business had grown dull, they lost all joy in it, and they failed."

You must have a good time meeting people if you expect them to have a good time meeting you.

I have asked thousands of business people to smile at someone every hour of the day for a week and then come to class and talk about the results. How did it work? Let's see...Here is a letter from William B. Steinhardt, a New York stockbroker. His case isn't isolated. In fact, it is typical of hundreds of cases.

"I have been married for over eighteen years," wrote Mr. Steinhardt, "and in all that time I seldom smiled at my wife or spoke two dozen words to her from the time I got up until I was ready to leave for business. I was one of the worst grouches who ever walked down Broadway.

"When you asked me to talk about my experience with smiles, I thought I would try it for a week. So the next morning, while combing my hair, I looked at my glum mug in the mirror and said to myself, 'Bill, you are going to wipe the scowl off that sour puss of yours today. You are going to smile. And you are going to begin right now.' As I sat down to breakfast, I greeted my wife with a 'Good morning, my dear,' and smiled as I said it.

"You warned me that she might be surprised. Well, you underestimated her reaction. She was bewildered. She was shocked. I told her that in the future she could expect this as a regular occurrence, and I kept it up every morning.

"This changed attitude of mine brought more happiness into our home in the two months since I started than there was during the last year.

"As I leave for my office, I greet the elevator operator in the apartment house with a 'Good morning' and a smile. I greet the doorman with a smile. I smile at the cashier in the subway booth when I ask for change. As I stand on the floor of the Stock Exchange, I smile at people who until recently never saw me smile.

"I soon found that everybody was smiling back at me. I treat those who come to me with complaints or grievances in a cheerful manner. I smile as I listen to them and I find that adjustments are accomplished much easier. I find that smiles are bringing me dollars, many dollars every day.

"I share my office with another broker. One of his clerks is a likable young chap, and I was so elated about the results I was getting that I told him recently about my new philosophy of human relations. He then confessed that when I first came to share my office with his firm he thought me a terrible grouch, and only recently changed his mind. He said I was really human when I smiled.

"I have also eliminated criticism from my system. I give appreciation and praise now instead of condemnation. I have stopped talking about what I want. I am now trying to see the other person's viewpoint. And these things have literally revolutionized my life. I am a totally different man, a happier man, a richer man, richer in friendships and happiness—the only things that matter much after all."

You don't feel like smiling? Then what? Two things. First, force yourself to smile. If you are alone, force yourself to whistle or hum a tune or sing. Act as if you were already happy, and that will tend to make you happy. Here is the way the psychologist and philosopher William James put it:

"Action seems to follow feeling, but really action and feeling go together; and by regulating the action, which is under the more direct control of the will, we can indirectly regulate the feeling, which is not.

"Thus the sovereign voluntary path to cheerfulness, if our cheerfulness be lost, is to sit up cheerfully and to act and speak as if cheerfulness were already there."

Everybody in the world is seeking happiness, and there is one sure way to find it. That is by controlling your thoughts. Happiness doesn't depend on outward conditions. It depends on inner conditions.

It isn't what you have or who you are or where you are or what you are doing that makes you happy or unhappy. It is what you think about it. For example, two people may be in the same place, doing the same thing; both may have about an equal amount of money and prestige, and yet one may be miserable and the other happy.

Why? Because of a different mental attitude. I have seen just as many happy faces among the poor peasants toiling with their primitive tools in the devastating heat of the tropics as I have seen in air-conditioned offices in New York, Chicago, or Los Angeles.

"There is nothing either good or bad," said Shakespeare, "but thinking makes it so."

Abe Lincoln once remarked that "most folks are about as happy as they make up their minds to be." He was right. I saw a vivid illustration of that truth as I was walking up the stairs of the Long Island Railroad station in New York. Directly in front of me thirty or forty crippled boys on canes and crutches were struggling up the stairs. One boy had to be carried up. I was astonished at their laughter and gaiety. I spoke about it to one of the men in charge of the boys. "Oh, yes," he said, "when a boy realizes that he is going to be a cripple for life, he is shocked at first; but after he gets over the shock, he usually resigns himself to his fate and then becomes as happy as normal boys."

I felt like taking my hat off to those boys. They taught me a lesson I hope I shall never forget.

Working all by oneself in a closed-off room in an office not only is lonely, but it denies one the opportunity of making friends with other employees in the company. Señora Maria Gonzalez of Guadalajara, Mexico, had such a job. She envied the shared comradeship of other people in the company as she heard their chatter and laughter. As she passed them in the hall during the first weeks of her employment, she shyly looked the other way.

After a few weeks, she said to herself, "Maria, you can't expect those women to come to you. You have to go out and meet them." The next time she walked to the water cooler, she put on her brightest smile and said, "Hi, how are you today?" to each of the people she met. The effect was immediate. Smiles and hellos were returned, the hallway seemed brighter, the job friendlier.

Acquaintanceships developed and some ripened into friendships. Her job and her life became more pleasant and interesting.

Peruse this bit of sage advice from the essayist and publisher Elbert Hubbard, but remember, perusing it won't do you any good unless you apply it:

Whenever you go out-of-doors, draw the chin in, carry the crown of the head high, and fill the lungs to the utmost; drink in the sunshine; greet your friends with a smile, and put soul into every handclasp. Do not fear being misunderstood and do not waste a minute thinking about your enemies. Try to fix firmly in your mind what you would like to do; and then, without veering off direction, you will move straight to the goal. Keep your mind on the great and splendid things you would like to do, and then, as the days go gliding away, you will find yourself unconsciously seizing upon the opportunities that are required for the fulfillment of your desire, just as the coral insect takes from the running tide the element it needs. Picture in your mind the able, earnest, useful person you desire to be, and the thought you hold is hourly transforming you into that particular individual... Thought is supreme. Preserve a right mental attitude—the attitude of courage, frankness, and good cheer. To think rightly is to create. All things come through desire and every sincere prayer is answered. We become like that on which our hearts are fixed. Carry your chin in and the crown of your head high. We are gods in the chrysalis.

The ancient Chinese were a wise lot—wise in the ways of the world; and they had a proverb that you and I ought to cut out and paste inside our hats. It goes like this: "A man without a smiling face must not open a shop."

Your smile is a messenger of your goodwill. Your smile brightens the lives of all who see it. To someone who has seen a dozen people frown, scowl or turn their faces away, your smile is like the sun breaking through the clouds. Especially when that someone is under pressure from his bosses, his customers, his teachers or parents or children, a smile can help him realize that all is not hopeless—that there is joy in the world.

Some years ago, a department store in New York City, in recognition of the pressures its sales clerks were under during the Christmas rush, presented the readers of its advertisements with the following homely philosophy:

【 THE VALUE OF A SMILE AT CHRISTMAS 】

It costs nothing, but creates much.

It enriches those who receive, without impoverishing those who give.

It happens in a flash and the memory of it sometimes lasts forever.

None are so rich they can get along without it, and none so poor but are richer for its benefits.

It creates happiness in the home, fosters goodwill in a business, and is the countersign of friends.

It is rest to the weary, daylight to the discouraged, sunshine to the sad, and Nature's best antidote for trouble.

Yet it cannot be bought, begged, borrowed, or stolen, for it is something that is no earthly good to anybody till it is given away.

And if in the last-minute rush of Christmas buying some of our salespeople should be too tired to give you a smile, may we ask you to leave one of yours?

For nobody needs a smile so much as those who have none left to give!

⇒ PRINCIPLE 2 ⇐

Smile.

↣ 6 ↢

"IF YOU DON'T DO THIS, YOU ARE HEADED FOR TROUBLE."

Back in 1898, a tragic thing happened in Rockland County, New York. A child had died, and on this particular day the neighbors were preparing to go to the funeral.

Jim Farley went out to the barn to hitch up his horse. The ground was covered with snow, the air was cold and snappy; the horse hadn't exercised for days; and as he was led out to the watering trough, he wheeled playfully, kicked both his heels high in the air, and killed Jim Farley. So the little village of Stony Point had two funerals that week instead of one.

Jim Farley left behind him a widow and three boys, and a few hundred dollars in insurance.

His oldest boy, Jim, was ten, and he went to work in a brickyard, wheeling sand and pouring it into the molds and turning the brick on edge to be dried by the sun. This boy Jim never had a chance to get much education. But with his natural geniality, he had a flair for making people like him, so he went into politics, and as the years went by, he developed an uncanny ability for remembering people's names.

He never saw the inside of a high school; but before he was forty-six years of age, four colleges had honored him with degrees and he had become chairman of the Democratic National Committee and Postmaster General of the United States.

I once interviewed Jim Farley and asked him the secret of his success. He said, "Hard work," and I said, "Don't be funny."

He then asked me what I thought was the reason for his success. I replied, "I understand you can call ten thousand people by their first names."

"No, you are wrong," he said. "I can call fifty thousand people by their first names."

Make no mistake about it. That ability helped Mr. Farley put Franklin D. Roosevelt in the White House when he managed Roosevelt's campaign in 1932.

During the years that Jim Farley traveled as a salesman for a gypsum concern, and during the years that he held office as town clerk in Stony Point, he built up a system for remembering names.

In the beginning, it was a very simple one. Whenever he met a new acquaintance, he found out his or her complete name and some facts about his or her family, business, and political opinions. He fixed all these facts well in mind as part of the picture, and the next time he met that person, even if it was a year later, he was able to shake hands, inquire after the family, and ask about the hollyhocks in the backyard. No wonder he developed a following!

For months before Roosevelt's campaign for President began, Jim Farley wrote hundreds of letters a day to people all over the western and northwestern states. Then he hopped onto a train and in nineteen days covered twenty states and twelve thousand miles, traveling by buggy, train, automobile, and boat. He would drop into town, meet his people at lunch or breakfast, tea or dinner, and give them a "heart-to-heart talk." Then he'd dash off again on another leg of his journey.

As soon as he arrived back East, he wrote to one person in each town he had visited, asking for a list of all the guests to whom he had talked. The final list contained thousands and thousands of names; yet each person on that list was paid the subtle flattery of getting a personal letter from James Farley. These letters began with "Dear Bill" or "Dear Jane," and they were always signed "Jim".

Jim Farley discovered early in life that the average person is more interested in his or her own name than in all the other names on earth put together. Remember that name and call it easily, and you have paid a subtle and very effective compliment. But forget it or misspell it—and you have placed yourself at a sharp disadvantage. For example, I once organized a public-speaking course in Paris and sent form letters to all the American residents in the city. French typists with apparently little knowledge of English filled in the names and naturally they made blunders. One man, the manager of a large American bank in Paris, wrote me a scathing rebuke because his name had been misspelled.

Sometimes it is difficult to remember a name, particularly if it is hard to pronounce. Rather than even try to learn it, many people ignore it or call the person by an easy nickname. Sid Levy called on a customer for some time whose name was Nicodemus Papadoulos. Most people just called him "Nick." Levy told us, "I made a special effort to say his name over several times to myself before I made my call. When I greeted him by his full name, 'Good afternoon, Mr. Nicodemus Papadoulos,' he was shocked. For what seemed like several minutes there was no reply from him at all. Finally, he said with tears rolling down his cheeks, 'Mr. Levy, in all the fifteen years I have been in this country, nobody has ever made the effort to call me by my right name.'"

What was the reason for Andrew Carnegie's success?

He was called the Steel King; yet he himself knew little about the manufacture of steel. He had hundreds of people working for him who knew far more about steel than he did.

But he knew how to handle people, and that is what made him rich. Early in life, he showed a flair for organization, a genius for leadership. By the time he was ten, he too had discovered the astounding importance people place on their own name. And he used that discovery to win cooperation. To illustrate: When he was a boy back in Scotland, he got hold of a rabbit, a mother rabbit. Presto! He soon had a whole nest of little rabbits—and nothing to feed them. But he had a brilliant idea. He told the boys and girls in the neighborhood that if they would go out and pull enough clover and dandelions to feed the rabbits, he would name the bunnies in their honor.

The plan worked like magic, and Carnegie never forgot it.

Years later, he made millions by using the same psychology in business. For example, he wanted to sell steel rails to the Pennsylvania

Railroad. J. Edgar Thomson was the president of the Pennsylvania Railroad then. So Andrew Carnegie built a huge steel mill in Pittsburgh and called it the "Edgar Thomson Steel Works."

Here is a riddle. See if you can guess it. When the Pennsylvania Railroad needed steel rails, where do you suppose J. Edgar Thomson bought them...from Sears, Roebuck? No. No. You're wrong. Guess again.

When Carnegie and George Pullman were battling each other for supremacy in the railroad sleeping-car business, the Steel King again remembered the lesson of the rabbits.

The Central Transportation Company, which Andrew Carnegie controlled, was fighting with the company that Pullman owned. Both were struggling to get the sleeping-car business of the Union Pacific Railroad, bucking each other, slashing prices, and destroying all chances of profit. Both Carnegie and Pullman had gone to New York to see the board of directors of the Union Pacific. Meeting one evening in the St. Nicholas Hotel, Carnegie said, "Good evening, Mr. Pullman, aren't we making a couple of fools of ourselves?"

"What do you mean?" Pullman demanded.

Then Carnegie expressed what he had on his mind—a merger of their two interests. He pictured in glowing terms the mutual advantages of working with, instead of against, each other. Pullman listened attentively, but he was not wholly convinced. Finally he asked, "What would you call the new company?" and Carnegie replied promptly, "Why, the Pullman Palace Car Company, of course."

Pullman's face brightened. "Come into my room," he said. "Let's talk it over." That talk made industrial history.

This policy of remembering and honoring the names of his friends and business associates was one of the secrets of Andrew Carnegie's leadership. He was proud of the fact that he could call many of his factory workers by their first names, and he boasted that while he was personally in charge, no strike ever disturbed his flaming steel mills.

Benton Love, chairman of Texas Commerce Bankshares, believes that the bigger a corporation gets, the colder it becomes. "One way to warm it up," he said, "is to remember people's names. The executive who tells me he can't remember names is at the same time telling me he can't remember a significant part of his business and is operating on quicksand."

Karen Kirsech of Rancho Palos Verdes, California, a flight attendant for TWA, made it a practice to learn the names of as many passengers in her cabin as possible and use the name when serving them. This resulted in many compliments on her service expressed both to her directly and to the airline. One passenger wrote, "I haven't flown TWA for some time, but I'm going to start flying nothing but TWA from now on. You make me feel that your airline has become a very personalized airline and that is important to me."

People are so proud of their names that they strive to perpetuate them at any cost. Even blustering, hard-boiled old P. T. Barnum, the greatest showman of his time, disappointed because he had no sons to carry on his name, offered his grandson, C. H. Seeley, $25,000 if he would call himself "Barnum" Seeley.

For many centuries, nobles and magnates supported artists, musicians, and authors so that their creative works would be dedicated to them.

Libraries and museums owe their richest collections to people who cannot bear to think that their names might perish from the memory of the race. The New York Public Library has its Astor and Lenox collections. The Metropolitan Museum perpetuates the names of Benjamin Altman and J. P. Morgan. And nearly every church is beautified by stained-glass windows commemorating the names of their donors. Many of the buildings on the campus of most universities bear the names of donors who contributed large sums of money for this honor.

Most people don't remember names, for the simple reason that they don't take the time and energy necessary to concentrate and repeat and fix names indelibly in their minds. They make excuses for themselves; they are too busy.

But they were probably no busier than Franklin D. Roosevelt, and he took time to remember and recall even the names of mechanics with whom he came into contact.

To illustrate: The Chrysler organization built a special car for Mr. Roosevelt, who could not use a standard car because his legs were paralyzed. W. F. Chamberlain and a mechanic delivered it to the White House. I have in front of me a letter from Mr. Chamberlain relating his experiences. "I taught President Roosevelt how to handle a car with a lot of unusual gadgets, but he taught me a lot about the fine art of handling people.

"When I called at the White House," Mr. Chamberlain writes, "the President was extremely pleasant and cheerful. He called me by name, made me feel very comfortable, and particularly impressed me with the fact that he was vitally interested in things I had to show him and tell him. The car was so designed that it could be operated entirely by hand. A crowd gathered around to look at the car; and he remarked, 'I think it is marvelous. All you have to do is to touch a button and it moves away and you can drive it without effort. I think it is grand—I don't know what makes it go. I'd love to have the time to tear it down and see how it works.'

"When Roosevelt's friends and associates admired the machine, he said in their presence: 'Mr. Chamberlain, I certainly appreciate all the time and effort you have spent in developing this car. It is a mighty fine job." He admired the radiator, the special rear-vision mirror and clock, the special spotlight, the kind of upholstery, the sitting position of the driver's seat, the special suitcases in the trunk with his monogram on each suitcase. In other words, he took notice of every detail to which he knew I had given considerable thought. He made a point of bringing these various pieces of equipment to the attention of Mrs. Roosevelt, Miss Perkins, the Secretary of Labor, and his secretary. He even brought the old White House porter into the picture by saying, 'George, you want to take particularly good care of the suitcases.'

"When the driving lesson was finished, the President turned to me and said: 'Well, Mr. Chamberlain, I have been keeping the Federal Reserve Board waiting thirty minutes. I guess I had better get back to work."

"I took a mechanic with me to the White House. He was introduced to Roosevelt when he arrived. He didn't talk to the President, and Roosevelt heard his name only once. He was a shy chap, and he kept in the background. But before leaving us, the President looked for the mechanic, shook his hand, called him by name, and thanked him for coming to Washington. And there was nothing perfunctory about his thanks. He meant what he said. I could feel that.

"A few days after returning to New York, I got an autographed photograph of President Roosevelt and a little note of thanks again expressing his appreciation for my assistance. How he found time to do it is a mystery to me."

Franklin D. Roosevelt knew that one of the simplest, most obvious and most important ways of gaining goodwill was by remembering names and making people feel important—yet how many of us do it?

Half the time we are introduced to a stranger, we chat for a few minutes and can't even remember his or her name by the time we say goodbye.

One of the first lessons a politician learns is this: "To recall a voter's name is statesmanship. To forget it is oblivion."

And the ability to remember names is almost as important in business and social contacts as it is in politics.

Napoleon III, Emperor of France and nephew of the great Napoleon, boasted that in spite of all his royal duties he could remember the name of every person he met.

His technique? Simple. If he didn't hear the name distinctly, he said, "So sorry. I didn't get the name clearly." Then, if it was an unusual name, he would say, "How is it spelled?"

During the conversation, he took the trouble to repeat the name several times, and tried to associate it in his mind with the person's features, expression, and general appearance.

If the person was someone of importance, Napoleon went to even further pains. As soon as His Royal Highness was alone, he wrote the name down on a piece of paper, looked at it, concentrated on it, fixed it securely in his mind, and then tore up the paper. In this way, he gained an eye impression of the name as well as an ear impression.

All this takes time, but "Good manners," said Emerson, "are made up of petty sacrifices."

The importance of remembering and using names is not just the prerogative of kings and corporate executives. It works for all of us. Ken Nottingham, an employee of General Motors in Indiana, usually had lunch at the company cafeteria. He noticed that the woman who worked behind the counter always had a scowl on her face. "She had been making sandwiches for about two hours and I was just another sandwich to her. I told her what I wanted. She weighed out the ham on a little scale, then she gave me one leaf of lettuce, a few potato chips and handed them to me.

"The next day I went through the same line. Same woman, same scowl. The only difference was I noticed her name tag. I smiled and said, 'Hello, Eunice,' and then told her what I wanted. Well, she forgot the scale, piled on the ham, gave me three leaves of lettuce and heaped on the potato chips until they fell off the plate."

We should be aware of the magic contained in a name and realize that this single item is wholly and completely owned by the person with whom we are dealing and nobody else. The name sets the individual apart; it makes him or her unique among all others. The information we are imparting or the request we are making takes on a special importance when we approach the situation with the name of the individual. From the waitress to the senior executive, the name will work magic as we deal with others.

⇒ PRINCIPLE 3 ⇐

Remember that a person's name is to that person the sweetest and most important sound in any language.

↣ 7 ↢

"AN EASY WAY TO BECOME A GOOD CONVERSATIONALIST."

Some time ago, I attended a bridge party. I don't play bridge, and there was a woman there who didn't play bridge either. She had discovered that I had once been Lowell Thomas' manager before he went on the radio and that I had traveled in Europe a great deal while helping him prepare the illustrated travel talks he was then delivering. So she said, "Oh, Mr. Carnegie, I do want you to tell me about all the wonderful places you have visited and the sights you have seen."

As we sat down on the sofa, she remarked that she and her husband had recently returned from a trip to Africa. "Africa!" I exclaimed. "How interesting! I've always wanted to see Africa, but I never got there except for a twenty-four-hour stay once in Algiers. Tell me, did you visit the big-game country? Yes? How fortunate. I envy you. Do tell me about Africa."

That kept her talking for forty-five minutes. She never again asked me where I had been or what I had seen. She didn't want to hear me talk about my travels. All she wanted was an interested listener, so she could expand her ego and tell about where she had been.

Was she unusual? No. Many people are like that.

For example, I met a distinguished botanist at a dinner party given by a New York book publisher. I had never talked with a botanist before, and I found him fascinating. I literally sat on the edge of my chair and listened while he spoke of exotic plants and experiments in developing new forms of plant life and indoor gardens (and even told me astonishing facts about the humble potato). I had a small indoor garden of my own, and he was good enough to tell me how to solve some of my problems.

As I said, we were at a dinner party. There must have been a dozen other guests, but I violated all the canons of courtesy, ignored everyone else, and talked for hours to the botanist.

Midnight came, I said good night to everyone and departed. The botanist then turned to our host and paid me several flattering compliments. I was "most stimulating". I was this and I was that, and he ended by saying I was a "most interesting conversationalist".

An interesting conversationalist? Why, I had hardly said anything at all. I couldn't have said anything if I had wanted to without changing the subject, for I didn't know any more about botany than I knew about the anatomy of a penguin. But I had done this: I had listened intently. I had listened because I was genuinely interested. And he felt it. Naturally that pleased him. That kind of listening is one of the highest compliments we can pay anyone. "Few human beings," wrote Jack Woodford in *Strangers in Love*, "few human beings are proof against the implied flattery of rapt attention." I went even further than giving him rapt attention. I was "hearty in my approbation and lavish in my praise."

I told him that I had been immensely entertained and instructed—and I had. I told him I wished I had his knowledge—and I did. I told him that I should love to wander the fields with him—and I have. I told him I must see him again—and I did.

And so I had him thinking of me as a good conversationalist when, in reality, I had been merely a good listener and had encouraged him to talk.

What is the secret, the mystery, of a successful business interview? Well, according to former Harvard president Charles W. Eliot, "There is no mystery about successful business intercourse... Exclusive attention to the person who is speaking to you is very important. Nothing else is so flattering as that."

Eliot himself was a past master of the art of listening. Henry James, one of America's first great novelists, recalled: "Dr. Eliot's listening was not mere silence, but a form of activity. Sitting very erect on the end of his spine with hands joined in his lap, making no movement except that he revolved his thumbs around each other faster or slower, he faced his interlocutor and seemed to be hearing with his eyes as well as his ears. He listened with his mind and attentively considered what you had to say while you said it. At the end of an interview the person who had talked to him felt that he had had his say."

Self-evident, isn't it? You don't have to study for four years in Harvard to discover that. Yet I know and you know department store owners who will rent expensive space, buy their goods economically, dress their windows appealingly, spend thousands of dollars in advertising and then hire clerks who haven't the sense to be good listeners—clerks who interrupt customers, contradict them, irritate them, and all but drive them from the store.

A department store in Chicago almost lost a regular customer who spent several thousand dollars each year in that store because a sales clerk wouldn't listen. Mrs. Henrietta Douglas, who took our course in Chicago, had purchased a coat at a special sale. After she had brought it home she noticed that there was a tear in the lining. She came back the next day and asked the sales clerk to exchange it. The clerk refused even to listen to her complaint. "You bought this at a special sale," she said. She pointed to a sign on the wall. "Read that," she exclaimed. "'All sales are final.' Once you buy it, you have to keep it. Sew up the lining yourself."

"But this was damaged merchandise," Mrs. Douglas complained.

"Makes no difference," the clerk interrupted. "Final's final."

Mrs. Douglas was about to walk out indignantly, swearing never to return to that store ever, when she was greeted by the department manager, who knew her from her many years of patronage. Mrs. Douglas told her what had happened.

The manager listened attentively to the whole story, examined the coat and then said, "Special sales are 'final' so we can dispose of merchandise at the end of the season. But this 'no return' policy does not apply to damaged goods. We will certainly repair or replace the lining, or if you prefer, give you your money back."

What a difference in treatment! If that manager had not come along and listened to the customer, a long-term patron of that store could have been lost forever.

Listening is just as important in one's home life as in the world of business. Millie Esposito of Croton-on-Hudson, New York, made it her business to listen carefully when one of her children wanted to speak with her. One evening she was sitting in the kitchen with her son, Robert, and after a brief discussion of something that was on his mind, Robert said, "Mom, I know that you love me very much."

Mrs. Esposito was touched and said, "Of course I love you very much. Did you doubt it?"

Robert responded, "No, but I really know you love me because whenever I want to talk to you about something you stop whatever you are doing and listen to me."

The chronic kicker, even the most violent critic, will frequently soften and be subdued in the presence of a patient, sympathetic listener—a listener who will be silent while the irate fault-finder dilates like a king cobra and spews the poison out of his system. To illustrate: The New York Telephone Company discovered a few years ago that it had to deal with one of the most vicious customers who ever cursed a customer service representative. And he did curse. He raved. He threatened to tear the phone out by its roots. He refused to pay certain charges that he declared were false. He wrote letters to the newspapers. He filed innumerable complaints with the Public Service Commission, and he started several suits against the telephone company.

At last, one of the company's most skillful 'troubleshooters' was sent to interview this stormy petrel. This "troubleshooter" listened and let the cantankerous customer enjoy himself pouring out his tirade. The telephone representative listened and said 'yes' and sympathized with his grievance.

"He raved on and I listened for nearly three hours," the 'troubleshooter' said as he related his experiences before one of the author's classes. "Then I went back and listened some more. I interviewed him four times, and before the fourth visit was over I had become a charter member of an organization he was starting. He called it the 'Telephone Subscribers' Protective Association.' I am still a member of this organization, and, so far as I know, I'm the only member in the world today besides Mr. ----.

"I listened and sympathized with him on every point that he made during these interviews. He had never had a telephone representative talk with him that way before, and he became almost friendly. The point on which I went to see him was not even mentioned on the first visit, nor was it mentioned on the second or third, but upon the fourth interview, I closed the case completely, he paid all his bills in full, and for the first time in the history of his difficulties with the telephone company he voluntarily withdrew his complaints from the Public Service Commission."

Doubtless Mr. ----- had considered himself a holy crusader, defending the public rights against callous exploitation. But in reality, what he had really wanted was a feeling of importance. He got this feeling of importance at first by kicking and complaining. But as soon as he got his feeling of importance from a representative of the company, his imagined grievances vanished into thin air.

One morning years ago, an angry customer stormed into the office of Julian F. Detmer, founder of the Detmer Woolen Company, which later became the world's largest distributor of woolens to the tailoring trade.

"This man owed us a small sum of money," Mr. Detmer explained to me. "The customer denied it, but we knew he was wrong. So our credit department had insisted that he pay. After getting a number of letters from our credit department, he packed his grip, made a trip to Chicago, and hurried into my office to inform me not only that he was not going to pay that bill, but that he was never going to buy another dollar's worth of goods from the Detmer Woolen Company.

"I listened patiently to all he had to say. I was tempted to interrupt, but I realized that would be bad policy, so I let him talk himself out. When he finally simmered down and got in a receptive mood, I said quietly, 'I want to thank you for coming to Chicago to tell me about this. You have done me a great favor, for if our credit department has annoyed you, it may annoy other good customers, and that would be just too bad. Believe me, I am far more eager to hear this than you are to tell it.'

"That was the last thing in the world he expected me to say. I think he was a trifle disappointed, because he had come to Chicago to tell me a thing or two, but here I was thanking him instead of scrapping with him. I assured him we would wipe the charge off the books and forget it, because he was a very careful man with only one account to look after, while our clerks had to look after thousands. Therefore, he was less likely to be wrong than we were.

"I told him that I understood exactly how he felt and that, if I were in his shoes, I would undoubtedly feel precisely as he did. Since he wasn't going to buy from us anymore, I recommended some other woolen houses.

"In the past, we had usually lunched together when he came to Chicago, so I invited him to have lunch with me today. He accepted reluctantly, but when we came back to the office he placed a larger order than ever before. He returned home in a softened mood and, wanting to be just as fair with us as we had been with him, looked over his bills, found one that had been mislaid, and sent us a check with his apologies.

"Later, when his wife presented him with a baby boy, he gave his son the middle name of Detmer, and he remained a friend and customer of the house until his death twenty-two years afterwards."

Years ago, a poor Dutch immigrant boy washed the windows of a bakery shop after school to help support his family. His people were so poor that in addition he used to go out in the street with a basket every day and collect stray bits of coal that had fallen in the gutter where the coal wagons had delivered fuel. That boy, Edward Bok, never got more than six years of schooling in his life; yet eventually he made himself one of the most successful magazine editors in the history of American journalism. How did he do it? That is a long story, but how he got his start can be told briefly. He got his start by using the principles advocated in this chapter.

He left school when he was thirteen and became an office boy for Western Union, but he didn't for one moment give up the idea of an education. Instead, he started to educate himself. He saved his car fares and went without lunch until he had enough money to buy an encyclopedia of American biography—and then he did an unheard-of thing. He read the lives of famous people and wrote to them asking for additional information about their childhoods. He was a good listener. He asked famous people to tell him more about themselves. He wrote General James A. Garfield, who was then running for President, and asked if it was true that he was once a towboy on a canal; and Garfield replied. He wrote General Grant asking about a certain battle, and Grant drew a map for him and invited this fourteen-year-old boy to dinner and spent the evening talking to him.

Soon our Western Union messenger boy was corresponding with many of the most famous people in the nation: Ralph Waldo Emerson, Oliver Wendell Holmes, Longfellow, Mrs. Abraham Lincoln, Louisa May Alcott, General Sherman and Jefferson Davis. Not only did he correspond with these distinguished people, but as soon as he got a vacation, he visited many of them as a welcome guest in their homes. This experience imbued him with a confidence that was invaluable. These men and women fired him with a vision and ambition that shaped his life. And all this, let me repeat, was made possible solely by the application of the principles we are discussing here.

Isaac F. Marcosson, a journalist who interviewed hundreds of celebrities, declared that many people fail to make a favorable impression because they don't listen attentively. "They have been so much concerned with what they are going to say next that they do not keep their ears open. Very important people have told me that they prefer good listeners to good talkers, but the ability to listen seems rarer than almost any other good trait."

And not only important personages crave a good listener, but ordinary folk do too. As the Reader's Digest once said, "Many people call a doctor when all they want is an audience."

During the darkest hours of the Civil War, Lincoln wrote to an old friend in Springfield, Illinois, asking him to come to Washington. Lincoln said he had some problems he wanted to discuss with him. The old neighbor called at the White House, and Lincoln talked to him for hours about the advisability of issuing a proclamation freeing the slaves. Lincoln went over all the arguments for and against such a move, and then read letters and newspaper articles, some denouncing him for not freeing the slaves and others denouncing him for fear he was going to free them. After talking for hours, Lincoln shook hands with his old neighbor, said good night, and sent him back to Illinois without even asking for his opinion. Lincoln had done all the talking himself. That seemed to clarify his mind. "He seemed to feel easier after that talk," the old friend said. Lincoln hadn't wanted advice. He had wanted merely a friendly, sympathetic listener to whom he could unburden himself. That's what we all want when we are in trouble. That is frequently all the irritated customer wants, and the dissatisfied employee or the hurt friend.

One of the great listeners of modern times was Sigmund Freud. A man who met Freud described his manner of listening, "It struck me so forcibly that I shall never forget him. He had qualities which I had never seen in any other man. Never had I seen such concentrated attention. There was none of that piercing 'soul-penetrating gaze' business. His eyes were mild and genial. His voice was low and kind. His gestures were few. But the attention he gave me, his appreciation of what I said, even when I said it badly, was extraordinary. *You've no idea what it meant to be listened to like that."*

If you want to know how to make people shun you and laugh at you behind your back and even despise you, here is the recipe: Never listen to anyone for long. Talk incessantly about yourself. If you have an idea while the other person is talking, don't wait for him or her to finish: burst right in and interrupt in the middle of a sentence.

Do you know people like that? I do, unfortunately; and the astonishing part of it is that some of them are prominent.

Bores, that is all they are—bores intoxicated with their own egos, drunk with a sense of their own importance.

People who talk only of themselves think only of themselves. And "those people who think only of themselves," Dr. Nicholas Murray Butler, long-time president of Columbia University, said, "are hopelessly uneducated. They are not educated," said Dr. Butler, "no matter how instructed they may be."

So if you aspire to be a good conversationalist, be an attentive listener. To be interesting, be interested. Ask questions that other persons will enjoy answering. Encourage them to talk about themselves and their accomplishments.

Remember that the people you are talking to are a hundred times more interested in themselves and their wants and problems than they are in you and your problems. A person's toothache means more to that person than a famine in China which kills a million people. A boil on one's neck interests one more than forty earthquakes in Africa. Think of that the next time you start a conversation.

⇒ PRINCIPLE 4 ⇐

Be a good listener. Encourage others to talk about themselves.

↣ 8 ↢

"HOW TO INTEREST PEOPLE."

**Everyone who was ever a guest of Theodore Roosevelt was astonished at the range and diversity of his knowledge. Whether his visitor was a cowboy or a Rough Rider, a New York politician or a diplomat, Roosevelt knew what to say. And how was it done? The answer was simple. Whenever Roosevelt expected a visitor, he sat up late the night before, reading up on the subject in which he knew his guest was particularly interested. For Roosevelt knew, as all leaders know, that the royal road to a person's heart is to talk about the things he or she treasures most. The genial William Lyon Phelps, essayist and professor of literature at Yale, learned this lesson early in life.

"When I was eight years old and was spending a weekend visiting my Aunt Libby Linsley at her home in Stratford on the Housatonic," he wrote in his essay on *Human Nature*, "a middle-aged man called one evening, and after a polite skirmish with my aunt, he devoted his attention to me. At that time, I happened to be excited about boats, and the visitor discussed the subject in a way that seemed to me particularly interesting. After he left, I spoke of him with enthusiasm. What a man! My aunt informed me he was a New York lawyer, that he cared nothing whatever about boats—that he took not the slightest interest in the subject. 'But why then did he talk all the time about boats?'

"'Because he is a gentleman. He saw you were interested in boats, and he talked about the things he knew would interest and please you. He made himself agreeable.'"

And William Lyon Phelps added, "I never forgot my aunt's remark."

As I write this chapter, I have before me a letter from Edward L. Chalif, who was active in Boy Scout work.

"One day I found I needed a favor," wrote Mr. Chalif. "A big Scout jamboree was coming off in Europe, and I wanted the president of one of the largest corporations in America to pay the expenses of one of my boys for the trip.

"Fortunately, just before I went to see this man, I heard that he had drawn a check for a million dollars, and that after it was canceled, he had had it framed.

"So the first thing I did when I entered his office was to ask to see the check. A check for a million dollars! I told him I never knew that anybody had ever written such a check, and that I wanted to tell my boys that I had actually seen a check for a million dollars. He gladly showed it to me; I admired it and asked him to tell me all about how it happened to be drawn."

You notice, don't you, that Mr. Chalif didn't begin by talking about the Boy Scouts, or the jamboree in Europe, or what it was he wanted? He talked in terms of what interested the other man. Here's the result:

"Presently, the man I was interviewing said, 'Oh, by the way, what was it you wanted to see me about?' So I told him.

"To my vast surprise," Mr. Chalif continues, "he not only immediately granted what I asked for, but much more. I had asked him to send only one boy to Europe, but he sent five boys and myself, gave me a letter of credit for a thousand dollars and told us to stay in Europe for seven weeks. He also gave me letters of introduction to his branch presidents, putting them at our service, and he himself met us in Paris and showed us the town.

Since then, he has given jobs to some of the boys whose parents were in need, and he is still active in our group.

"Yet I know if I hadn't found out what he was interested in, and got him warmed up first, I wouldn't have found him one-tenth as easy to approach."

Is this a valuable technique to use in business? Is it? Let's see. Take Henry G. Duvernoy of Duvernoy and Sons, a wholesale baking firm in New York.

Mr. Duvernoy had been trying to sell bread to a certain New York hotel. He had called on the manager every week for four years. He went to the same social affairs the manager attended. He even took rooms in the hotel and lived there in order to get the business. But he failed.

"Then," said Mr. Duvernoy, "after studying human relations, I resolved to change my tactics. I decided to find out what interested this man—what caught his enthusiasm.

"I discovered he belonged to a society of hotel executives called the Hotel Greeters of America. He not only belonged, but his bubbling enthusiasm had made him president of the organization, and president of the International Greeters. No matter where its conventions were held, he would be there.

"So when I saw him the next day, I began talking about the Greeters. What a response I got. What a response! He talked to me for half an hour about the Greeters, his tones vibrant with enthusiasm. I could plainly see that this society was not only his hobby; it was the passion of his life. Before I left his office, he had 'sold' me a membership in his organization.

"In the meantime, I had said nothing about bread. But a few days later, the steward of his hotel phoned me to come over with samples and prices.

"'I don't know what you did to the old boy,' the steward greeted me, 'but he sure is sold on you!'

"Think of it! I had been drumming at that man for four years—trying to get his business—and I'd still be drumming at him if I hadn't finally taken the trouble to find out what he was interested in, and what he enjoyed talking about."

Edward E. Harriman of Hagerstown, Maryland, chose to live in the beautiful Cumberland Valley of Maryland after he completed his military service. Unfortunately, at that time there were few jobs available in the area. A little research uncovered the fact that a number of companies in the area were either owned or controlled by an unusual business maverick, R. J. Funkhouser, whose rise from poverty to riches intrigued Mr. Harriman. However, he was known for being inaccessible to job seekers. Mr. Harriman wrote:

"I interviewed a number of people and found that his major interest was anchored in his drive for power and money. Since he protected himself from people like me by using a dedicated and stern secretary, I studied her interests and goals and only then I paid an unannounced visit to her office. She had been Mr. Funkhouser's orbiting satellite for about fifteen years. When I told her I had a proposition for him which might translate itself into financial and political success for him, she became enthused. I also conversed with her about her constructive participation in his success. After this conversation she arranged for me to meet Mr. Funkhouser.

"I entered his huge and impressive office determined not to ask directly for a job. He was seated behind a large carved desk and thundered at me, 'How about it, young man?' I said, 'Mr. Funkhouser, I believe I can make money for you.' He immediately rose and invited me to sit in one of the large upholstered chairs. I enumerated my ideas and the qualifications I had to realize these ideas, as well as how they would contribute to his personal success and that of his businesses.

"'R. J.', as he became known to me, hired me at once and for over twenty years I have grown in his enterprises and we both have prospered."

Talking in terms of the other person's interests pays off for both parties. Howard Z. Herzig, a leader in the field of employee communications, has always followed this principle. When asked what reward he got from it, Mr. Herzig responded that he not only received a different reward from each person but that in general the reward had been an enlargement of his life each time he spoke to someone.

⇒ PRINCIPLE 5 ⇐

Talk in terms of the other person's interests.

→ 9 ←

"HOW TO MAKE PEOPLE LIKE YOU INSTANTLY."

I was waiting in line to register a letter in the post office at Thirty-third Street and Eighth Avenue in New York. I noticed that the clerk appeared to be bored with the job—weighing envelopes, handing out stamps, making change, issuing receipts—the same monotonous grind year after year. So I said to myself, "I am going to try to make that clerk like me. Obviously, to make him like me, I must say something nice, not about myself, but about him. So I asked myself, 'What is there about him that I can honestly admire?'" That is sometimes a hard question to answer, especially with strangers; but, in this case, it happened to be easy. I instantly saw something I admired no end.

So while he was weighing my envelope, I remarked with enthusiasm, "I certainly wish I had your head of hair."

He looked up, half-startled, his face beaming with smiles. "Well, it isn't as good as it used to be," he said modestly. I assured him that although it might have lost some of its pristine glory, nevertheless it was still magnificent. He was immensely pleased. We carried on a pleasant little conversation and the last thing he said to me was: "Many people have admired my hair."

I'll bet that person went out to lunch that day walking on air. I'll bet he went home that night and told his wife about it. I'll bet he looked in the mirror and said, "It is a beautiful head of hair."

I told this story once in public and a man asked me afterward, "What did you want to get out of him?"

What was I trying to get out of him!!! What was I trying to get out of him!!!

If we are so contemptibly selfish that we can't radiate a little happiness and pass on a bit of honest appreciation without trying to get something out of the other person in return—if our souls are no bigger than sour crab apples, we shall meet with the failure we so richly deserve. Oh yes, I did want something out of that chap. I wanted something priceless. And I got it. I got the feeling that I had done something for him without his being able to do anything whatever in return for me. That is a feeling that flows and sings in your memory long after the incident is past.

There is one all-important law of human conduct. If we obey that law, we shall almost never get into trouble. In fact, that law, if obeyed, will bring us countless friends and constant happiness. But the very instant we break the law, we shall get into endless trouble. The law is this: Always make the other person feel important. John Dewey, as we have already noted, said that the desire to be important is the deepest urge in human nature; and William James said, "The deepest principle in human nature is the craving to be appreciated." As I have already pointed out, it is this urge that differentiates us from the animals. It is this urge that has been responsible for civilization itself.

Philosophers have been speculating on the rules of human relationships for thousands of years, and out of all that speculation, there has evolved only one important precept. It is not new. It is as old as history. Zoroaster taught it to his followers in Persia twenty-five hundred years ago. Confucius preached it in China twenty-four centuries ago. Lao-tse, the founder of Taoism, taught it to his disciples in the Valley of the Han. Buddha preached it on the bank of the Holy Ganges five hundred years before Christ. The sacred books of Hinduism taught it a thousand years before that. Jesus taught it among the stony hills of Judea nineteen centuries ago. Jesus summed it up in one thought—probably the most important rule in the world: "Do unto others as you would have others do unto you."

You want the approval of those with whom you come in contact. You want recognition of your true worth. You want a feeling that you are important in your little world. You don't want to listen to cheap, insincere flattery, but you do crave sincere appreciation. You want your friends and associates to be, as Charles Schwab put it, "hearty in their approbation and lavish in their praise." All of us want that.

So let's obey the Golden Rule, and give unto others what we would have others give unto us. How? When? Where? The answer is: All the time, everywhere.

David G. Smith of Eau Claire, Wisconsin, told one of our classes how he handled a delicate situation when he was asked to take charge of the refreshment booth at a charity concert. "The night of the concert I arrived at the park and found two elderly ladies in a very bad humor standing next to the refreshment stand. Apparently each thought that she was in charge of this project. As I stood there pondering what to do, one of the members of the sponsoring committee appeared and handed me a cashbox and thanked me for taking over the project. She introduced Rose and Jane as my helpers and then ran off.

"A great silence ensued. Realizing that the cash box was a symbol of authority (of sorts), I gave the box to Rose and explained that I might not be able to keep the money straight and that if she took care of it I would feel better. I then suggested to Jane that she show two teenagers who had been assigned to refreshments how to operate the soda machine, and I asked her to be responsible for that part of the project.

"The evening was very enjoyable with Rose happily counting the money, Jane supervising the teenagers, and me enjoying the concert."

You don't have to wait until you are ambassador to France or chairman of the Clambake Committee of your lodge before you use this philosophy of appreciation. You can work magic with it almost every day.

If, for example, the waitress brings us mashed potatoes when we have ordered French fries, let's say, "I'm sorry to trouble you, but I prefer French fries." She'll probably reply, "No trouble at all," and will be glad to change the potatoes, because we have shown respect for her.

Little phrases such as "I'm sorry to trouble you," "Would you be so kind as to...?" "Won't you please?" "Would you mind?" "Thank you"—little courtesies like these oil the cogs of the monotonous grind of everyday life—and, incidentally, they are the hallmark of good breeding.

Let's take another illustration. Hall Caine's novels—The Christian, The Deemster, The Manxman, among them—were all best-sellers in the early part of this century. Millions of people read his novels, countless millions. He was the son of a blacksmith. He never had more than eight years' schooling in his life; yet when he died he was the richest literary man of his time.

The story goes like this: Hall Caine loved sonnets and ballads; so he devoured all of Dante Gabriel Rossetti's poetry. He even wrote a lecture chanting the praises of Rossetti's artistic achievement and sent a copy to Rossetti himself. Rossetti was delighted. "Any young man who has such an exalted opinion of my ability," Rossetti probably said to himself, "must be brilliant." So Rossetti invited this blacksmith's son to come to London and act as his secretary. That was the turning point in Hall Caine's life; for, in his new position, he met the literary artists of the day. Profiting by their advice and inspired by their encouragement, he launched upon a career that emblazoned his name across the sky.

His home, Greeba Castle, on the Isle of Man, became a Mecca for tourists from the far corners of the world, and he left a multimillion-dollar estate. Yet—who knows—he might have died poor and unknown had he not written an essay expressing his admiration for a famous man.

Such is the power, the stupendous power, of sincere, heartfelt appreciation.

Rossetti considered himself important. That is not strange. Almost everyone considers himself important, very important.

The life of many people could probably be changed if only someone would make him feel important. Ronald J. Rowland, who is one of the instructors of our course in California, is also a teacher of arts and crafts. He wrote to us about a student named Chris in his beginning crafts class:

"Chris was a very quiet, shy boy lacking in self-confidence, the kind of student that often does not receive the attention he deserves. I also teach an advanced class that has grown to be somewhat of a status symbol and a privilege for a student to have earned the right to be in it. On Wednesday, Chris was diligently working at his desk. I really felt there was a hidden fire deep inside him. I asked Chris if he would like to be in the advanced class. How I wish I could express the look in Chris's face, the emotions in that shy fourteen-year-old boy, trying to hold back his tears."

"Who me, Mr. Rowland? Am I good enough?"

"Yes, Chris, you are good enough."

I had to leave at that point because tears were coming to my eyes. As Chris walked out of class that day, seemingly two inches taller, he looked at me with bright blue eyes and said in a positive voice, "Thank you, Mr. Rowland."

Chris taught me a lesson I will never forget—our deep desire to feel important. To help me never forget this rule, I made a sign which reads "YOU ARE IMPORTANT." This sign hangs in the front of the classroom for all to see and to remind me that each student I face is equally important.

The unvarnished truth is that almost all the people you meet feel superior to you in some way, and a sure way to their hearts is to let them realize in some subtle way that you recognize their importance, and recognize it sincerely.

Remember what Emerson said, "Every man I meet is my superior in some way. In that, I learn of him."

And the pathetic part of it is that frequently those who have the least justification for a feeling of achievement bolster up their egos by a show of tumult and conceit which is truly nauseating. As Shakespeare put it, "...man, proud man,/Dressed in a little brief authority,/...Plays such fantastic tricks before high heaven/As make the angels weep."

I am going to tell you how business people in my own courses have applied these principles with remarkable results. Let's take the case of a Connecticut attorney (because of his relatives he prefers not to have his name mentioned).

Shortly after joining the course, Mr. R----- drove to Long Island with his wife to visit some of her relatives. She left him to chat with an old aunt of hers and they rushed off by themselves to visit some of the younger relatives. Since he soon had to give a speech professionally on how he applied the principles of appreciation, he thought he would gain some worthwhile experience talking with the elderly lady. So he looked around the house to see what he could honestly admire.

"This house was built about 1890, wasn't it?" he inquired.

"Yes," she replied, "that is precisely the year it was built."

"It reminds me of the house I was born in," he said. "It's beautiful. Well-built. Roomy. You know, they don't build houses like this anymore."

"You're right," the old lady agreed. "The young folks nowadays don't care for beautiful homes. All they want is a small apartment, and then they go off gadding about in their automobiles.

"This is a dream house," she said in a voice vibrating with tender memories. "This house was built with love. My husband and I dreamed about it for years before we built it. We didn't have an architect. We planned it all ourselves."

She showed Mr. R----- about the house, and he expressed his hearty admiration for the beautiful treasures she had picked up in her travels and cherished over a lifetime—paisley shawls, an old English tea set, Wedgwood china, French beds and chairs, Italian paintings, and silk draperies that had once hung in a French chateau.

After showing Mr. R----- through the house, she took him out to the garage. There, jacked up on blocks, was a Packard car—in mint condition.

"My husband bought that car for me shortly before he passed on," she said softly. "I have never ridden in it since his death...You appreciate nice things, and I'm going to give this car to you."

"Why, Aunty," he said, "you overwhelm me. I appreciate your generosity, of course; but I couldn't possibly accept it. I'm not even a relative of yours. I have a new car, and you have many relatives that would like to have that Packard."

"Relatives!" she exclaimed. "Yes, I have relatives who are just waiting till I die so they can get that car. But they are not going to get it."

"If you don't want to give it to them, you can very easily sell it to a secondhand dealer," he told her.

"Sell it!" she cried. "Do you think I would sell this car? Do you think I could stand to see strangers riding up and down the street in that car—that car that my husband bought for me? I wouldn't dream of selling it. I'm going to give it to you. You appreciate beautiful things."

He tried to get out of accepting the car, but he couldn't without hurting her feelings.

This lady, left all alone in a big house with her paisley shawls, her French antiques, and her memories, was starving for a little recognition. She had once been young and beautiful and sought after. She had once built a house warm with love and had collected things from all over Europe to make it beautiful. Now, in the isolated loneliness of old age, she craved a little human warmth, a little genuine appreciation—and no one gave it to her. And when she found it, like a spring in the desert, her gratitude couldn't adequately express itself with anything less than the gift of her cherished Packard.

Let's take another case: Donald M. McMahon, who was superintendent of Lewis and Valentine, nurserymen and landscape architects in Rye, New York, related this incident:

"Shortly after I attended the talk on 'How to Win Friends and Influence People,' I was landscaping the estate of a famous attorney. The owner came out to give me a few instructions about where he wished to plant a mass of rhododendrons and azaleas.

"I said, 'Judge, you have a lovely hobby. I've been admiring your beautiful dogs. I understand you win a lot of blue ribbons every year at the show in Madison Square Garden.'

"The effect of this little expression of appreciation was striking.

"'Yes,' the judge replied, 'I do have a lot of fun with my dogs. Would you like to see my kennel?'

"He spent almost an hour showing me his dogs and the prizes they had won. He even brought out their pedigrees and explained about the bloodlines responsible for such beauty and intelligence.

"Finally, turning to me, he asked, 'Do you have any small children?'

"'Yes, I do,' I replied, 'I have a son.'

"'Well, wouldn't he like a puppy?' the judge inquired.

"'Oh, yes, he'd be tickled pink.'

"'All right, I'm going to give him one,' the judge announced.

"He started to tell me how to feed the puppy. Then he paused. 'You'll forget it if I tell you. I'll write it out.' So the judge went into the house, typed out the pedigree and feeding instructions, and gave me a puppy worth several hundred dollars and one hour and fifteen minutes of his valuable time largely because I had expressed my honest admiration for his hobby and achievements."

George Eastman, of Kodak fame, invented the transparent film that made motion pictures possible, amassed a fortune of a hundred million dollars, and made himself one of the most famous businessmen on earth. Yet in spite of all these tremendous accomplishments, he craved little recognition even as you and I.

To illustrate: When Eastman was building the Eastman School of Music and also Kilbourn Hall in Rochester, James Adamson, then president of the Superior Seating Company of New York, wanted to get the order to supply the theater chairs for these buildings. Phoning the architect, Mr. Adamson made an appointment to see Mr. Eastman in Rochester.

When Adamson arrived, the architect said, "I know you want to get this order, but I can tell you right now that you won't stand a ghost of a show if you take more than five minutes of George Eastman's time. He is a strict disciplinarian. He is very busy. So tell your story quickly and get out."

Adamson was prepared to do just that.

When he was ushered into the room he saw Mr. Eastman bending over a pile of papers at his desk. Presently, Mr. Eastman looked up, removed his glasses, and walked toward the architect and Mr. Adamson, saying, "Good morning, gentlemen, what can I do for you?"

The architect introduced them, and then Mr. Adamson said, "While we've been waiting for you, Mr. Eastman, I've been admiring your office. I wouldn't mind working in a room like this myself. I'm in the interior-woodworking business, and I never saw a more beautiful office in all my life."

George Eastman replied, "You remind me of something I had almost forgotten. It is beautiful, isn't it? I enjoyed it a great deal when it was first built. But I come down here now with a lot of other things on my mind and sometimes don't even see the room for weeks at a time."

Adamson walked over and rubbed his hand across a panel. "This is English oak, isn't it? A little different texture from Italian oak."

"Yes," Eastman replied. "Imported English oak. It was selected for me by a friend who specializes in fine woods."

Then Eastman showed him about the room, commenting on the proportions, the coloring, the hand carving and other effects he had helped to plan and execute.

While drifting about the room, admiring the woodwork, they paused before a window, and George Eastman, in his modest, soft-spoken way, pointed out some of the institutions through which he was trying to help humanity: the University of Rochester, the General Hospital, the Homeopathic Hospital, the Friendly Home, the Children's Hospital. Mr. Adamson congratulated him warmly on the idealistic way he was using his wealth to alleviate the sufferings of humanity. Presently, George Eastman unlocked a glass case and pulled out the first camera he had ever owned—an invention he had bought from an Englishman.

Adamson questioned him at length about his early struggles to get started in business, and Mr. Eastman spoke with real feeling about the poverty of his childhood, telling how his widowed mother had kept a boardinghouse while he clerked in an insurance office. The terror of poverty haunted him day and night, and he resolved to make enough money so that his mother wouldn't have to work. Mr. Adamson drew him out with further questions and listened, absorbed, while he related the story of his experiments with dry photographic plates. He told how he had worked in an office all day, and sometimes experimented all night, taking only brief naps while the chemicals were working, sometimes working and sleeping in his clothes for seventy-two hours at a stretch.

James Adamson had been ushered into Eastman's office at ten-fifteen and had been warned that he must not take more than five minutes; but an hour had passed, then two hours passed. And they were still talking. Finally, George Eastman turned to Adamson and said, "The last time I was in Japan I bought some chairs, brought them home, and put them on my sun porch. But the sun peeled the paint, so I went downtown the other day and bought some paint and painted the chairs myself. Would you like to see what sort of a job I can do painting chairs? All right. Come up to my home and have lunch with me and I'll show you."

After lunch, Mr. Eastman showed Adamson the chairs he had brought from Japan. They weren't worth more than a few dollars, but George Eastman, now a multimillionaire, was proud of them because he himself had painted them.

The order for the seats amounted to $90,000. Who do you suppose got the order—James Adamson or one of his competitors?

From the time of this story until Mr. Eastman's death, he and James Adamson were close friends.

Claude Marais, a restaurant owner in Rouen, France, used this principle and saved his restaurant from the loss of a key employee. This woman had been in his employ for five years and was a vital link between M. Marais and his staff of twenty-one people. He was shocked to receive a registered letter from her advising him of her resignation.

M. Marais reported, "I was very surprised and, even more, disappointed, because I was under the impression that I had been fair to her and receptive to her needs. As much as she was a friend as well as an employee, I probably had taken her too much for granted and maybe was even more demanding of her than of other employees.

"I could not, of course, accept this resignation without some explanation. I took her aside and said, 'Paulette, you must understand that I cannot accept your resignation. You mean a great deal to me and to this company, and you are as important to the success of this restaurant as I am.' I repeated this in front of the entire staff, and I invited her to my home and reiterated my confidence in her with my family present.

"Paulette withdrew her resignation, and today I can rely on her as never before. I frequently reinforce this by expressing my appreciation for what she does and showing her how important she is to me and to the restaurant."

"Talk to people about themselves," said Disraeli, one of the shrewdest men who ever ruled the British Empire. "Talk to people about themselves and they will listen for hours."

⇒ PRINCIPLE 6 ⇐

Make the other person feel important—and do it sincerely.

In a Nutshell

SIX WAYS TO MAKE PEOPLE LIKE YOU

⇒ PRINCIPLE 1 ⇐

Become genuinely interested in other people.

⇒ PRINCIPLE 2 ⇐

Smile.

⇒ PRINCIPLE 3 ⇐

Remember that a person's name is to that person the sweetest and most important sound in any language.

⇒ PRINCIPLE 4 ⇐

Be a good listener. Encourage others to talk about themselves.

⇒ PRINCIPLE 5 ⇐

Talk in terms of the other person's interests.

⇒ PRINCIPLE 6 ⇐

Make the other person feel important—and do it sincerely.

PART THREE

How To Win People To Your Way Of Thinking

↣ 10 ↢

"YOU CAN'T WIN AN ARGUMENT."

Shortly after the close of World War I, I learned an invaluable lesson one night in London. I was manager at the time for Sir Ross Smith. During the war, Sir Ross had been the Australian ace out in Palestine; and shortly after peace was declared, he astonished the world by flying halfway around it in thirty days. No such feat had ever been attempted before. It created a tremendous sensation. The Australian government awarded him fifty thousand dollars; the King of England knighted him; and, for a while, he was the most talked-about man under the Union Jack. I was attending a banquet one night given in Sir Ross's honor; and during the dinner, the man sitting next to me told a humorous story which hinged on the quotation "There's a divinity that shapes our ends, rough-hew them how we will."

The raconteur mentioned that the quotation was from the Bible. He was wrong. I knew that. I knew it positively. There couldn't be the slightest doubt about it. And so, to get a feeling of importance and display my superiority, I appointed myself as an unsolicited and unwelcome committee of one to correct him. He stuck to his guns. What? From Shakespeare? Impossible! Absurd! That quotation was from the Bible. And he knew it.

The storyteller was sitting on my right; and Frank Gammond, an old friend of mine, was seated at my left. Mr. Gammond had devoted years to the study of Shakespeare. So the storyteller and I agreed to submit the question to Mr. Gammond. Mr. Gammond listened, kicked me under the table, and then said: "Dale, you are wrong. The gentleman is right. It is from the Bible."

On our way home that night, I said to Mr. Gammond, "Frank, you knew that quotation was from Shakespeare,"

"Yes, of course," he replied, "*Hamlet*, Act Five, Scene Two. But we were guests at a festive occasion, my dear Dale. Why prove to a man he is wrong? Is that going to make him like you? Why not let him save his face? He didn't ask for your opinion. He didn't want it. Why argue with him? Always avoid the acute angle."

The man who said that taught me a lesson I'll never forget. I not only had made the storyteller uncomfortable, but had put my friend in an embarrassing situation. How much better it would have been had I not become argumentative.

It was a sorely needed lesson because I had been an inveterate arguer. During my youth, I had argued with my brother about everything under the Milky Way. When I went to college, I studied logic and argumentation and went in for debating contests. Talk about being from Missouri, I was born there. I had to be shown. Later, I taught debating and argumentation in New York; and once, I am ashamed to admit, I planned to write a book on the subject. Since then, I have listened to, engaged in, and watched the effect of thousands of arguments. As a result of all this, I have come to the conclusion that there is only one way under high heaven to get the best of an argument—and that is to avoid it.

Avoid it as you would avoid rattlesnakes and earthquakes.

Nine times out of ten, an argument ends with each of the contestants more firmly convinced than ever that he is absolutely right.

You can't win an argument. You can't because if you lose it, you lose it; and if you win it, you lose it. Why? Well, suppose you triumph over the other man and shoot his argument full of holes and prove that he is non compos mentis. Then what? You will feel fine. But what about him? You have made him feel inferior. You have hurt his pride. He will resent your triumph. And...

A man convinced against his will is of the same opinion still.

Years ago Patrick J. O'Haire joined one of my classes. He had had little education, and how he loved a scrap! He had once been a chauffeur, and he came to me because he had been trying, without much success, to sell trucks. A little questioning brought out the fact that he was continually scrapping with and antagonizing the very people he was trying to do business with. If a prospect said anything derogatory about the trucks he was selling, Pat saw red and was right at the customer's throat. Pat won a lot of arguments in those days. As he said to me afterward, "I often walked out of an office saying, 'I told that bird something.' Sure I had told him something, but I hadn't sold him anything."

My first problem was not to teach Patrick J. O'Haire to talk. My immediate task was to train him to refrain from talking and to avoid verbal fights.

Mr. O'Haire became one of the star salesmen for the White Motor Company in New York. How did he do it? Here is his story in his own words: "If I walk into a buyer's office now and he says, 'What? A White truck? They're no good! I wouldn't take one if you gave it to me. I'm going to buy the Whose-It truck,' I say, 'The Whose-It is a good truck. If you buy the Whose-It, you'll never make a mistake. The Whose-Its are made by a fine company and sold by good people.'

"He is speechless then. There is no room for an argument. If he says the Whose-It is best and I say sure it is, he has to stop. He can't keep on talking all afternoon saying, 'It's the best' when I agree with him. We then get off the subject of Whose-It and I begin to talk about the good points of the White truck.

"There was a time when a remark like his first one would have made me see scarlet and red and orange. I would start arguing against Whose-It; and the more I argued against it, the more my prospect argued in favor of it; and the more he argued, the more he sold himself on my competitor's product.

"As I look back now I wonder how I was ever able to sell anything. I lost years of my life in scrapping and arguing. I keep my mouth shut now. It pays."

As wise old Ben Franklin used to say: If you argue and rankle and contradict, you may achieve a victory sometimes; but it will be an empty victory because you will never get your opponent's good will.

So figure it out for yourself. Which would you rather have, an academic, theatrical victory or a person's good will? You can seldom have both.

The Boston Transcript once printed this bit of significant doggerel:

Here lies the body of William Jay,
Who died maintaining his right of way—
He was right, dead right, as he sped along,
But he's just as dead as if he were wrong.

You may be right, dead right, as you speed along in your argument; but as far as changing another's mind is concerned, you will probably be just as futile as if you were wrong.

Frederick S. Parsons, an income tax consultant, had been arguing and wrangling for an hour with a government tax inspector. An item of nine thousand dollars was at stake. Mr. Parsons claimed that this nine thousand dollars was in reality a bad debt, that it would never be collected, that it ought not to be taxed. "Bad debt, my eye!" retorted the inspector. "It must be taxed."

"This inspector was cold, arrogant and stubborn," Mr. Parsons said as he told the story to the class. "Reason was wasted and so were facts...The longer we argued, the more stubborn he became. So I decided to avoid arguments, change the subject, and give him appreciation.

"I said, 'I suppose this is a very petty matter in comparison with the really important and difficult decisions you're required to make. I've made a study of taxation myself. But I've had to get my knowledge from books. You are getting yours from the firing line of experience. I sometimes wish I had a job like yours. It would teach me a lot.' I meant every word I said.

"Well." The inspector straightened up in his chair, leaned back, and talked for a long time about his work, telling me of the clever frauds he had uncovered. His tone gradually became friendly, and presently he was telling me about his children. As he left, he advised me that he would consider my problem further and give me his decision in a few days.

"He called at my office three days later and informed me that he had decided to leave the tax return exactly as it was filed."

This tax inspector was demonstrating one of the most common human frailties. He wanted a feeling of importance; and as long as Mr. Parsons argued with him, he got his feeling of importance by loudly asserting his authority. But as soon as his importance was admitted and the argument stopped and he was permitted to expand his ego, he became a sympathetic and kindly human being.

Buddha said, "Hatred is never ended by hatred but by love," and a misunderstanding is never ended by an argument but by tact, diplomacy, conciliation and a sympathetic desire to see the other person's viewpoint.

Lincoln once reprimanded a young army officer for indulging in a violent controversy with an associate. "No man who is resolved to make the most of himself," said Lincoln, "can spare time for personal contention. Still less can he afford to take the consequences, including the vitiation of his temper and the loss of self-control. Yield larger things to which you show no more than equal rights; and yield lesser ones though clearly your own. Better give your path to a dog than be bitten by him in contesting for the right. Even killing the dog would not cure the bite."

In an article in *Bits and Pieces**, some suggestions are made on how to keep a disagreement from becoming an argument:

Welcome to the disagreement. Remember the slogan, "When two partners always agree, one of them is not necessary." If there is some point you haven't thought about, be thankful if it is brought to your attention. Perhaps this disagreement is your opportunity to be corrected before you make a serious mistake.

Distrust your first instinctive impression. Our first natural reaction in a disagreeable situation is to be defensive. Be careful. Keep calm and watch out for your first reaction. It may be you at your worst, not your best.

Control your temper. Remember, you can measure the size of a person by what makes him or her angry.

Listen first. Give your opponents a chance to talk. Let them finish. Do not resist, defend or debate. This only raises barriers. Try to build bridges of understanding. Don't build higher barriers of misunderstanding.

Look for areas of agreement. When you have heard your opponents out, dwell first on the points and areas on which you agree.

Be honest. Look for areas where you can admit error and say so. Apologize for your mistakes. It will help disarm your opponents and reduce defensiveness.

Promise to think over your opponents' ideas and study them carefully. And mean it. Your opponents may be right. It is a lot easier at this stage to agree to think about their points than to move rapidly ahead and find yourself in a position where your opponents can say, "We tried to tell you, but you wouldn't listen."

Thank your opponents sincerely for their interest. Anyone who takes the time to disagree with you is interested in the same things you are. Think of them as people who really want to help you, and you may turn your opponents into friends.

Postpone action to give both sides time to think through the problem. Suggest that a new meeting be held later that day or the next day, when all the facts may be brought to bear. In preparation for this meeting, ask yourself some hard questions:

Could my opponents be right? Partly right? Is there truth or merit in their position or argument? Is my reaction one that will relieve the problem, or will it just relieve any frustration? Will my reaction drive my opponents further away or draw them closer to me? Will my reaction elevate the estimation good people have of me? Will I win or lose? What price will I have to pay if I win? If I am quiet about it, will the disagreement blow over? Is this difficult situation an opportunity for me?

* *Bits and Pieces*, published by The Economics Press, Fairfield, N.J.

Opera tenor Jan Peerce, after he was married nearly fifty years, once said, "My wife and I made a pact a long time ago, and we've kept it no matter how angry we've grown with each other. When one yells, the other should listen, because when two people yell, there is no communication, just noise and bad vibrations."

⇒ PRINCIPLE 1 ⇐

The only way to get the best of an argument is to avoid it.

↣ 11 ↢

"A SURE WAY OF MAKING ENEMIES—AND HOW TO AVOID IT."

When Theodore Roosevelt was in the White House, he confessed that if he could be right 75 percent of the time, he would reach the highest measure of his expectation.

If that was the highest rating that one of the most distinguished men of the twentieth century could hope to obtain, what about you and me?

If you can be sure of being right only 55 percent of the time, you can go down to Wall Street and make a million dollars a day. If you can't be sure of being right even 55 percent of the time, why should you tell other people they are wrong?

You can tell people they are wrong by a look or an intonation or a gesture just as eloquently as you can in words—and if you tell them they are wrong, do you make them want to agree with you? Never! For you have struck a direct blow at their intelligence, judgment, pride and self-respect. That will make them want to strike back. But it will never make them want to change their minds. You may then hurl at them all the logic of a Plato or an Immanuel Kant, but you will not alter their opinions, for you have hurt their feelings.

Never begin by announcing "I am going to prove so-and-so to you." That's bad. That's tantamount to saying, "I'm smarter than you are, I'm going to tell you a thing or two and make you change your mind."

That is a challenge. It arouses opposition and makes the listener want to battle with you before you even start.

It is difficult, under even the most benign conditions, to change people's minds. So why make it harder? Why handicap yourself?

If you are going to prove anything, don't let anybody know it. Do it so subtly, so adroitly, that no one will feel that you are doing it. This was expressed succinctly by Alexander Pope: Men must be taught as if you taught them not, and things unknown proposed as things forgot.

Over three hundred years ago Galileo said, "You cannot teach a man anything; you can only help him to find it within himself."

As Lord Chesterfield said to his son, "Be wiser than other people if you can, but do not tell them so."

Socrates said repeatedly to his followers in Athens, "One thing only I know, and that is that I know nothing."

Well, I can't hope to be any smarter than Socrates, so I have quit telling people they are wrong. And I find that it pays.

If a person makes a statement that you think is wrong—yes, even that you know is wrong—isn't it better to begin by saying, "Well, now, look, I thought otherwise, but I may be wrong. I frequently am. And if I am wrong, I want to be put right. Let's examine the facts."

There's magic, positive magic, in such phrases as, "I may be wrong. I frequently am. Let's examine the facts."

Nobody in the heavens above or on earth beneath or in the waters under the earth will ever object to your saying, "I may be wrong. Let's examine the facts."

One of our class members who used this approach in dealing with customers was Harold Reinke, a Dodge dealer in Billings, Montana. He reported that because of the pressures of the automobile business, he was often hard-boiled and callous when dealing with customers' complaints. This caused flared tempers, loss of business and general unpleasantness.

He told his class, "Recognizing that this was getting me nowhere fast, I tried a new tack. I would say something like this, 'Our dealership has made so many mistakes that I am frequently ashamed. We may have erred in your case. Tell me about it.'"

"This approach becomes quite disarming, and by the time the customer releases his feelings, he is usually much more reasonable when it comes to settling the matter. In fact, several customers have thanked me for having such an understanding attitude. And two of them have even brought in friends to buy new cars. In this highly competitive market, we need more of this type of customer, and I believe that showing respect for all customers' opinions and treating them diplomatically and courteously will help beat the competition."

You will never get into trouble by admitting that you may be wrong. That will stop all arguments and inspire your opponent to be just as fair and open and broad-minded as you are. It will make him want to admit that he, too, may be wrong.

If you know positively that a person is wrong, and you bluntly tell him or her so, what happens? Let me illustrate. Mr. S----, a young New York attorney, once argued a rather important case before the United States Supreme Court (Lustgarten v. Fleet Corporation, 280 U.S. 320). The case involved a considerable sum of money and an important question of law. During the argument, one of the Supreme Court Justices said to him, "The statute of limitations in admiralty law is six years, is it not?"

Mr. S---- stopped, stared at the Justice for a moment, and then said bluntly, "Your Honor, there is no statute of limitations in admiralty."

"A hush fell on the court," said Mr. S---- as he related his experience to one of the author's classes, "and the temperature in the room seemed to drop to zero. I was right. Justice—was wrong. And I had told him so. But did that make him friendly? No. I still believe that I had the law on my side. And I know that I spoke better than I ever spoke before. But I wasn't persuaded. I made the enormous blunder of telling a very learned and famous man that he was wrong."

Few people are logical. Most of us are prejudiced and biased. Most of us are blighted with preconceived notions, with jealousy, suspicion, fear, envy and pride. And most citizens don't want to change their minds about their religion or their haircut or communism or their favorite movie star. So, if you are inclined to tell people they are wrong, please read the following paragraph every morning before breakfast. It is from James Harvey Robinson's enlightening book The Mind in the Making.

We sometimes find ourselves changing our minds without any resistance or heavy emotion, but if we are told we are wrong, we resent the imputation and harden our hearts. We are incredibly heedless in the formation of our beliefs, but find ourselves filled with an illicit passion for them when anyone proposes to rob us of their companionship. It is obviously not the ideas themselves that are dear to us, but our self-esteem which is threatened...The little word 'my' is the most important one in human affairs, and properly to reckon with it is the beginning of wisdom. It has the same force whether it is 'my' dinner, 'my' dog, and 'my' house, or 'my' father, 'my' country, and 'my' God. We not only resent the imputation that our watch is wrong, or our car shabby, but that our conception of the canals of Mars, of the pronunciation of "Epictetus", of the medicinal value of salicin, or of the date of Sargon I is subject to revision. We like to continue to believe what we have been accustomed to accept as true, and the resentment aroused when doubt is cast upon any of our assumptions leads us to seek every manner of excuse for clinging to it. The result is that most of our so-called reasoning consists in finding arguments for going on believing as we already do.

Carl Rogers, the eminent psychologist, wrote in his book On Becoming a Person:

I have found it of enormous value when I can permit myself to understand the other person. The way in which I have worded this statement may seem strange to you. Is it necessary to permit oneself to understand another? I think it is. Our first reaction to most of the statements (which we hear from other people) is an evaluation or judgment, rather than an understanding of it. When someone expresses some feeling, attitude or belief, our tendency is almost immediately to feel "that's right," or "that's stupid," "that's abnormal," "that's unreasonable," "that's incorrect," "that's not nice." Very rarely do we permit ourselves to understand precisely what the meaning of the statement is to the other person.*

* Adapted from Carl R. Rogers, On Becoming a Person (Boston: Houghton Mifflin, 1961), pp. 18ff.

I once employed an interior decorator to make some draperies for my home. When the bill arrived, I was dismayed.

A few days later, a friend dropped in and looked at the draperies. The price was mentioned, and she exclaimed with a note of triumph, "What? That's awful. I am afraid he put one over on you."

True? Yes, she had told the truth, but few people like to listen to truths that reflect on their judgment. So, being human, I tried to defend myself. I pointed out that the best is eventually the cheapest, that one can't expect to get quality and artistic taste at bargain-basement prices, and so on and on.

The next day another friend dropped in, admired the draperies, bubbled over with enthusiasm, and expressed a wish that she could afford such exquisite creations for her home. My reaction was totally different.

"Well, to tell the truth," I said, "I can't afford them myself. I paid too much. I'm sorry I ordered them."

When we are wrong, we may admit it to ourselves. And if we are handled gently and tactfully, we may admit it to others and even take pride in our frankness and broad-mindedness. But not if someone else is trying to ram the unpalatable fact down our esophagus.

Horace Greeley, the most famous editor in America during the time of the Civil War, disagreed violently with Lincoln's policies. He believed that he could drive Lincoln into agreeing with him by a campaign of argument, ridicule and abuse. He waged this bitter campaign month after month, year after year. In fact, he wrote a brutal, bitter, sarcastic and personal attack on President Lincoln the night Booth shot him.

But did all this bitterness make Lincoln agree with Greeley? Not at all. Ridicule and abuse never do. If you want some excellent suggestions about dealing with people and managing yourself and improving your personality, read Benjamin Franklin's autobiography—one of the most fascinating life stories ever written, one of the classics of American literature. Ben Franklin tells how he conquered the iniquitous habit of argument and transformed himself into one of the most able, suave and diplomatic men in American history.

One day, when Ben Franklin was a blundering youth, an old Quaker friend took him aside and lashed him with a few stinging truths, something like this:

Ben, you are impossible. Your opinions have a slap in them for everyone who differs with you. They have become so offensive that nobody cares for them. Your friends find they enjoy themselves better when you are not around. You know so much that no man can tell you anything. Indeed, no man is going to try, for the effort would lead only to discomfort and hard work. So you are not likely ever to know any more than you do now, which is very little.

One of the finest things I know about Ben Franklin is the way he accepted that smarting rebuke. He was big enough and wise enough to realize that it was true, to sense that he was headed for failure and social disaster. So he made a right-about-face. He began immediately to change his insolent, opinionated ways.

"I made it a rule," said Franklin, "to forbear all direct contradiction to the sentiment of others, and all positive assertion of my own. I even forbade myself the use of every word or expression in the language that imported a fix'd opinion, such as 'certainly,' 'undoubtedly,' etc., and I adopted, instead of them, 'I conceive,' 'I apprehend,' or 'I imagine' a thing to be so or so, or 'it so appears to me at present.' When another asserted something that I thought an error, I deny'd myself the pleasure of contradicting him abruptly, and of showing immediately some absurdity in his proposition: and in answering I began by observing that in certain cases or circumstances his opinion would be right, but in the present case there appear'd or seem'd to me some difference, etc. I soon found the advantage of this change in my manner; the conversations I engag'd in went on more pleasantly. The modest way in which I propos'd my opinions procur'd them a readier reception and less contradiction; I had less mortification when I was found to be in the wrong, and I more easily prevaile'd with others to give up their mistakes and join with me when I happened to be in the right.

"And this mode, which I at first put on with some violence to natural inclination, became at length so easy, and so habitual to me, that perhaps for these fifty years past no one has ever heard a dogmatical expression escape me. And to this habit (after my character of integrity) I think it principally owing that I had earned so much weight with my fellow citizens when I proposed new institutions, or alterations in the old, and so much influence in public councils when I became a member; for I was but a bad speaker, never eloquent, subject to much hesitation in my choice of words, hardly correct in language, and yet I generally carried my points."

How do Ben Franklin's methods work in business? Let's take two examples.

Katherine A. Allred of Kings Mountain, North Carolina, is an industrial engineering supervisor for a yarn-processing plant. She told one of our classes how she handled a sensitive problem before and after taking our training:

"Part of my responsibility," she reported, "deals with setting up and maintaining incentive systems and standards for our operators so they can make more money by producing more yarn. The system we were using had worked fine when we had only two or three different types of yarn, but recently we had expanded our inventory and capabilities to enable us to run more than twelve different varieties. The present system was no longer adequate to pay the operator by the class of yarn she was running at any one particular time. With my new system in hand, I entered the meeting determined to prove to the management that my system was the right approach. I told them in detail how they were wrong and showed where they were being unfair and how I had all the answers they needed. To say the least, I failed miserably! I had become so busy defending my position on the new system that I had left them no opening to graciously admit their problems on the old one. The issue was dead.

"After several sessions of this course, I realized all too well where I had made my mistakes. I called another meeting and this time I asked where they felt their problems were. We discussed each point, and I asked them their opinions on which was the best way to proceed. With a few low-keyed suggestions, at proper intervals, I let them develop my system themselves. At the end of the meeting when I actually presented my system, they enthusiastically accepted it.

"I am convinced now that nothing good is accomplished and a lot of damage can be done if you tell a person straight out that he or she is wrong. You only succeed in stripping that person of self-dignity and making yourself an unwelcome part of any discussion."

Let's take another example—and remember these cases I am citing are typical of the experiences of thousands of other people. R. V. Crowley was a salesman for a lumber company in New York. Crowley admitted that he had been telling hard-boiled lumber inspectors for years that they were wrong. And he had won the arguments too. But it hadn't done any good. "For these lumber inspectors," said Mr. Crowley, "are like baseball umpires. Once they make a decision, they never change it."

Mr. Crowley saw that his firm was losing thousands of dollars through the arguments he won. So while taking my course, he resolved to change tactics and abandon arguments. With what results? Here is the story as he told it to the fellow members of his class:

"One morning the phone rang in my office. A hot and bothered person at the other end proceeded to inform me that a car of lumber we had shipped into his plant was entirely unsatisfactory. His firm had stopped unloading and requested that we make immediate arrangements to remove the stock from their yard. After about one-fourth of the car had been unloaded, their lumber inspector reported that the lumber was running 55 percent below grade. Under the circumstances, they refused to accept it.

"I immediately started for his plant and on the way turned over in my mind the best way to handle the situation. Ordinarily, under such circumstances, I should have quoted grading rules and tried, as a result of my own experience and knowledge as a lumber inspector, to convince the other inspector that the lumber was actually up to grade, and that he was misinterpreting the rules in his inspection. However, I thought I would apply the principles learned in this training.

"When I arrived at the plant, I found the purchasing agent and the lumber inspector in a wicked mood, both set for an argument and a fight. We walked out to the car that was being unloaded, and I requested that they continue to unload so that I could see how things were going. I asked the inspector to go right ahead and lay out the rejects, as he had been doing, and to put the good pieces in another pile.

"After watching him for a while it began to dawn on me that his inspection actually was much too strict and that he was misinterpreting the rules. This particular lumber was white pine, and I knew the inspector was thoroughly schooled in hardwoods but not a competent, experienced inspector on white pine. White pine happened to be my own strong suit, but did I offer any objection to the way he was grading the lumber? None whatsoever. I kept on watching and gradually began to ask questions as to why certain pieces were not satisfactory. I didn't for one instant insinuate that the inspector was wrong. I emphasized that my only reason for asking was in order that we could give his firm exactly what they wanted in future shipments.

"By asking questions in a very friendly, cooperative spirit, and insisting continually that they were right in laying out boards not satisfactory to their purpose, I got him warmed up, and the strained relations between us began to thaw and melt away. An occasional carefully put remark on my part gave birth to the idea in his mind that possibly some of these rejected pieces were actually within the grade that they had bought, and that their requirements demanded a more expensive grade. I was very careful, however, not to let him think I was making an issue of this point.

"Gradually his whole attitude changed. He finally admitted to me that he was not experienced on white pine and began to ask me questions about each piece as it came out of the car. I would explain why such a piece came within the grade specified, but kept on insisting that we did not want him to take it if it was unsuitable for their purpose. He finally got to the point where he felt guilty every time he put a piece in the rejected pile. And at last he saw that the mistake was on their part for not having specified as good a grade as they needed.

"The ultimate outcome was that he went through the entire carload again after I left, accepted the whole lot, and we received a check in full.

"In that one instance alone, a little tact, and the determination to refrain from telling the other man he was wrong, saved my company a substantial amount of cash, and it would be hard to place a money value on the goodwill that was saved."

Martin Luther King was asked how, as a pacifist, he could be an admirer of Air Force General Daniel "Chappie" James, then the nation's highest-ranking black officer. Dr. King replied, "I judge people by their own principles—not by my own."

In a similar way, General Robert E. Lee once spoke to the President of the Confederacy, Jefferson Davis, in the most glowing terms about a certain officer under his command. Another officer in attendance was astonished. "General," he said, "do you not know that the man of whom you speak so highly is one of your bitter enemies who misses no opportunity to malign you?" "Yes," replied General Lee, "but the President asked my opinion of him; he did not ask for his opinion of me."

By the way, I am not revealing anything new in this chapter. Two thousand years ago, Jesus said: "Agree with thine adversary quickly."

And 2,200 years before Christ was born, King Akhtoli of Egypt gave his son some shrewd advice—advice that is sorely needed today. "Be diplomatic," counseled the King. "It will help you gain your point."

In other words, don't argue with your customer or your spouse or your adversary. Don't tell them they are wrong, don't get them stirred up. Use a little diplomacy.

⇒ PRINCIPLE 2 ⇐

Show respect for the other person's opinions. Never say, "You're wrong."

↣ 12 ↢

"IF YOU'RE WRONG, ADMIT IT."

Within a minute's walk of my house there was a wild stretch of virgin timber, where the blackberry thickets foamed white in the springtime, where the squirrels nested and reared their young, and the horseweeds grew as tall as a horse's head. This unspoiled woodland was called Forest Park—and it was a forest, probably not much different in appearance from what it was when Columbus discovered America. I frequently walked in this park with Rex, my little Boston bulldog. He was a friendly, harmless little hound; and since we rarely met anyone in the park, I took Rex along without a leash or a muzzle.

One day we encountered a mounted policeman in the park, a policeman itching to show his authority. "What do you mean by letting that dog run loose in the park without a muzzle and leash?" he reprimanded me. "Don't you know it's against the law?" "Yes, I know it is," I replied softly, "but I didn't think he would do any harm out here." "You didn't think! You didn't think so! The law doesn't give a tinker's damn about what you think. That dog might kill a squirrel or bite a child. Now, I'm going to let you off this time; but if I catch this dog out here again without a muzzle and a leash, you'll have to tell it to the judge." I meekly promised to obey.

And I did obey—for a few times. But Rex didn't like the muzzle, and neither did I; so we decided to take a chance. Everything was lovely for a while, and then we struck a snag. Rex and I raced over the brow of a hill one afternoon and there, suddenly—to my dismay—I saw the majesty of the law, astride a bay horse. Rex was out in front, heading straight for the officer.

I was in for it. I knew it. So I didn't wait until the policeman started talking. I beat him to it. I said: "Officer, you've caught me red-handed. I'm guilty. I have no alibis, no excuses. You warned me last week that if I brought the dog out here again without a muzzle you would fine me." "Well, now," the policeman responded in a soft tone. "I know it's a temptation to let a little dog like that have a run out here when nobody is around." "Sure it's a temptation," I replied, "but it is against the law." "Well, a little dog like that isn't going to harm anybody," the policeman remonstrated. "No, but he may kill squirrels," I said. "Well now, I think you are taking this a bit too seriously," he told me. "I'll tell you what you do. You just let him run over the hill there where I can't see him—and we'll forget all about it."

That policeman, being human, wanted a feeling of importance; so when I began to condemn myself, the only way he could nourish his self-esteem was to take the magnanimous attitude of showing mercy.

But suppose I had tried to defend myself—well, did you ever argue with a policeman?

But instead of breaking lances with him, I admitted that he was absolutely right and I was absolutely wrong; I admitted it quickly, openly, and with enthusiasm. The affair terminated graciously in my taking his side and his taking my side. Lord Chesterfield himself could hardly have been more gracious than this mounted policeman, who, only a week previously, had threatened to have the law on me.

If we know we are going to be rebuked anyhow, isn't it far better to beat the other person to it and do it ourselves? Isn't it much easier to listen to self-criticism than to bear condemnation from alien lips?

Say about yourself all the derogatory things you know the other person is thinking or wants to say or intends to say—and say them before that person has a chance to say them. The chances are a hundred to one that a generous, forgiving attitude will be taken and your mistakes will be minimized just as the mounted policeman did with me and Rex.

Ferdinand E. Warren, a commercial artist, used this technique to win the goodwill of a petulant, scolding buyer of art.

"It is important, in making drawings for advertising and publishing purposes, to be precise and very exact," Mr. Warren said as he told the story.

"Some art editors demand that their commissions be executed immediately; and in these cases, some slight error is liable to occur. I knew one art director in particular who was always delighted to find fault with some little thing. I have often left his office in disgust, not because of the criticism, but because of his method of attack. Recently I delivered a rush job to this editor, and he phoned me to call at his office immediately. He said something was wrong. When I arrived, I found just what I had anticipated—and dreaded. He was hostile, gloating over his chance to criticize. He demanded with heat why I had done so-and-so. My opportunity had come to apply the self-criticism I had been studying about. So I said, 'Mr. So-and-so, if what you say is true, I am at fault and there is absolutely no excuse for my blunder. I have been doing drawings for you long enough to know better. I'm ashamed of myself.'"

"Immediately he started to defend me. 'Yes, you're right, but after all, this isn't a serious mistake. It is only...'"

"I interrupted him. 'Any mistake,' I said, 'may be costly and they are all irritating.'"

"He started to break in, but I wouldn't let him. I was having a grand time. For the first time in my life, I was criticizing myself—and I loved it."

"'I should have been more careful,' I continued. 'You give me a lot of work, and you deserve the best; so I'm going to do this drawing all over.'"

"'No! No!' he protested. 'I wouldn't think of putting you to all that trouble.' He praised my work, assured me that he wanted only a minor change and that my slight error hadn't cost his firm any money; and, after all, it was a mere detail—not worth worrying about."

"My eagerness to criticize myself took all the fight out of him. He ended up by taking me to lunch; and before we parted, he gave me a check and another commission."

There is a certain degree of satisfaction in having the courage to admit one's errors. It not only clears the air of guilt and defensiveness, but often helps solve the problem created by the error.

Bruce Harvey of Albuquerque, New Mexico, had incorrectly authorized payment of full wages to an employee on sick leave. When he discovered his error, he brought it to the attention of the employee and explained that to correct the mistake he would have to reduce his next paycheck by the entire amount of the overpayment. The employee pleaded that as that would cause him a serious financial problem, could the money be repaid over a period of time? In order to do this, Harvey explained, he would have to obtain his supervisor's approval. "And this I knew," reported Harvey, "would result in a boss-type explosion. While trying to decide how to handle this situation better, I realized that the whole mess was my fault and I would have to admit it to my boss."

"I walked into his office, told him that I had made a mistake and then informed him of the complete facts. He replied in an explosive manner that it was the fault of the personnel department. I repeated that it was my fault. He exploded again about carelessness in the accounting department. Again I explained it was my fault. He blamed two other people in the office. But each time I reiterated it was my fault. Finally, he looked at me and said, 'Okay, it was your fault. Now straighten it out.' The error was corrected and nobody got into trouble. I felt great because I was able to handle a tense situation and had the courage not to seek alibis. My boss has had more respect for me ever since."

Any fool can try to defend his or her mistakes—and most fools do—but it raises one above the herd and gives one a feeling of nobility and exultation to admit one's mistakes. For example, one of the most beautiful things that history records about Robert E. Lee is the way he blamed himself and only himself for the failure of Pickett's charge at Gettysburg.

Pickett's charge was undoubtedly the most brilliant and picturesque attack that ever occurred in the Western world. General George E. Pickett himself was picturesque. He wore his hair so long that his auburn locks almost touched his shoulders; and, like Napoleon in his Italian campaigns, he wrote ardent love letters almost daily while on the battlefield. His devoted troops cheered him that tragic July afternoon as he rode off jauntily toward the Union lines, his cap set at a rakish angle over his right ear. They cheered and they followed him, man touching man, rank pressing rank, with banners flying and bayonets gleaming in the sun. It was a gallant sight. Daring. Magnificent. A murmur of admiration ran through the Union lines as they beheld it.

Pickett's troops swept forward at an easy trot, through orchards and cornfields, across a meadow and over a ravine. All the time, the enemy's cannon was tearing ghastly holes in their ranks. But on they pressed, grim, irresistible.

Suddenly the Union infantry rose from behind the stone wall on Cemetery Ridge where they had been hiding and fired volley after volley into Pickett's onrushing troops. The crest of the hill was a sheet of flame, a slaughterhouse, a blazing volcano. In a few minutes, all of Pickett's brigade commanders except one were down, and four-fifths of his five thousand men had fallen.

General Lewis A. Armistead, leading the troops in the final plunge, ran forward, vaulted over the stone wall, and, waving his cap on the top of his sword, shouted: "Give 'em the steel, boys!"

They did. They leaped over the wall, bayoneted their enemies, smashed skulls with clubbed muskets, and planted the battle flags of the South on Cemetery Ridge. The banners waved there only for a moment. But that moment, brief as it was, recorded the high-water mark of the Confederacy.

Pickett's charge—brilliant, heroic—was nevertheless the beginning of the end. Lee had failed. He could not penetrate the North. And he knew it.

The South was doomed.

Lee was so saddened, so shocked, that he sent in his resignation and asked Jefferson Davis, the President of the Confederacy, to appoint "a younger and abler man." If Lee had wanted to blame the disastrous failure of Pickett's charge on someone else, he could have found a score of alibis. Some of his division commanders had failed him. The cavalry hadn't arrived in time to support the infantry attack. This had gone wrong and that had gone awry.

But Lee was far too noble to blame others. As Pickett's beaten and bloody troops struggled back to the Confederate lines, Robert E. Lee rode out to meet them all alone and greeted them with a self-condemnation that was little short of sublime. "All this has been my fault," he confessed. "I and I alone have lost this battle."

Few generals in all history have had the courage and character to admit that.

Michael Cheung, who teaches our course in Hong Kong, told of how Chinese culture presents some special problems and how sometimes it is necessary to recognize that the benefit of applying a principle may be more advantageous than maintaining an old tradition. He had one middle-aged class member who had been estranged from his son for many years. The father had been an opium addict, but was now cured. In Chinese tradition an older person cannot take the first step. The father felt that it was up to his son to take the initiative toward a reconciliation. In an early session, he told the class about the grandchildren he had never seen and how much he desired to be reunited with his son. His classmates, all Chinese, understood his conflict between his desire and long-established tradition. The father felt that young people should have respect for their elders and that he was right in not giving in to his desire, but to wait for his son to come to him.

Toward the end of the course the father again addressed his class. "I have pondered this problem," he said. "Dale Carnegie says, 'If you are wrong, admit it quickly and emphatically.' It is too late for me to admit it quickly, but I can admit it emphatically. I wronged my son. He was right in not wanting to see me and to expel me from his life. I may lose face by asking a younger person's forgiveness, but I was at fault and it is my responsibility to admit this." The class applauded and gave him their full support. At the next class he told how he went to his son's house, asked for and received forgiveness and was now embarked on a new relationship with his son, his daughter-in-law and the grandchildren he had at last met.

Elbert Hubbard was one of the most original authors who ever stirred up a nation, and his stinging sentences often aroused fierce resentment. But Hubbard with his rare skill for handling people frequently turned his enemies into friends.

For example, when some irritated reader wrote in to say that he didn't agree with such-and-such an article and ended by calling Hubbard this and that, Elbert Hubbard would answer like this:

"Come to think it over, I don't entirely agree with it myself. Not everything I wrote yesterday appeals to me today. I am glad to learn what you think on the subject. The next time you are in the neighborhood you must visit us and we'll get this subject threshed out for all time. So here is a handclasp over the miles, and I am,

Yours sincerely,
Elbert Hubbard"

What could you say to a man who treated you like that?

When we are right, let's try to win people gently and tactfully to our way of thinking, and when we are wrong—and that will be surprisingly often, if we are honest with ourselves—let's admit our mistakes quickly and with enthusiasm. Not only will that technique produce astonishing results; but, believe it or not, it is a lot more fun, under the circumstances, than trying to defend oneself.

Remember the old proverb: "By fighting you never get enough, but by yielding you get more than you expected."

⇒ PRINCIPLE 3 ⇐

If you are wrong, admit it quickly and emphatically.

↣ 13 ↢

"A DROP OF HONEY."

If your temper is aroused and you tell 'em a thing or two, you will have a fine time unloading your feelings. But what about the other person? Will he share your pleasure? Will your belligerent tones, your hostile attitude, make it easy for him to agree with you?

"If you come at me with your fists doubled," said Woodrow Wilson, "I think I can promise you that mine will double as fast as yours; but if you come to me and say, 'Let us sit down and take counsel together, and, if we differ from each other, understand why it is that we differ, just what the points at issue are,' we will presently find that we are not so far apart after all, that the points on which we differ are few and the points on which we agree are many, and that if we only have the patience and the candor and the desire to get together, we will get together."

Nobody appreciated the truth of Woodrow Wilson's statement more than John D. Rockefeller, Jr. Back in 1915, when Rockefeller was the most fiercely despised man in Colorado, one of the bloodiest strikes in the history of American industry had been shocking the state for two terrible years. Irate, belligerent miners were demanding higher wages from the Colorado Fuel and Iron Company; Rockefeller controlled that company. Property had been destroyed; troops had been called out. Blood had been shed. Strikers had been shot, their bodies riddled with bullets.

At a time like that, with the air seething with hatred, Rockefeller wanted to win the strikers to his way of thinking. And he did it. How? Here's the story. After weeks spent in making friends, Rockefeller addressed the representatives of the strikers. This speech, in its entirety, is a masterpiece. It produced astonishing results. It calmed the tempestuous waves of hate that threatened to engulf Rockefeller. It won him a host of admirers. It presented facts in such a friendly manner that the strikers went back to work without saying another word about the increase in wages for which they had fought so violently.

The opening of that remarkable speech follows. Note how it fairly glows with friendliness. Rockefeller, remember, was talking to men who, a few days previously, had wanted to hang him by the neck to a sour apple tree; yet he couldn't have been more gracious, more friendly if he had addressed a group of medical missionaries. His speech was radiant with such phrases as "I am proud to be here", "having visited in your homes", "met many of your wives and children," "we meet here not as strangers, but as friends", "spirit of mutual friendship", "our common interests", "it is only by your courtesy that I am here", etc.

"This is a red-letter day in my life," Rockefeller began. "It is the first time I have had the good fortune to meet the representatives of the employees of this great company, its officers and superintendents, together, and I can assure you that I am proud to be here, and that I shall remember this gathering as long as I live. Had this meeting been held two weeks ago, I would have stood here a stranger to most of you, recognizing a few faces. Having had the opportunity last week of visiting all the camps in the southern coal field and of talking individually with practically all of the representatives, except those who were away; having visited in your homes, met many of your wives and children, we meet here not as strangers, but as friends, and it is in that spirit of mutual friendship that I am glad to have this opportunity to discuss with you our common interests.

"Since this is a meeting of the officers of the company and the representatives of the employees, it is only by your courtesy that I am here, for I am not so fortunate as to be either one or the other; and yet I feel that I am intimately associated with you men, for, in a sense, I represent both the stockholders and the directors."

Isn't that a superb example of the fine art of making friends out of enemies?

Suppose Rockefeller had taken a different tack. Suppose he had argued with those miners and hurled devastating facts in their faces. Suppose he had told them by his tones and insinuations that they were wrong. Suppose that, by all the rules of logic, he had proved that they were wrong. What would have happened? More anger would have been stirred up, more hatred, more revolt.

If a man's heart is rankling with discord and ill feeling toward you, you can't win him to your way of thinking with all the logic in Christendom. Scolding parents and domineering bosses and husbands and nagging wives ought to realize that people don't want to change their minds. They can't be forced or driven to agree with you or me. But they may possibly be led to, if we are gentle and friendly, ever so gentle and ever so friendly.

Lincoln said that, in effect, over a hundred years ago. Here are his words: "It is an old and true maxim that 'a drop of honey catches more flies than a gallon of gall.' So with men, if you would win a man to your cause, first convince him that you are his sincere friend. Therein is a drop of honey that catches his heart; which, say what you will, is the great high road to his reason."

Business executives have learned that it pays to be friendly to strikers. For example, when 2,500 employees in the White Motor Company's plant struck for higher wages and a union shop, Robert F. Black, then president of the company, didn't lose his temper and condemn and threaten and talk of tyranny and Communists. He actually praised the strikers. He published an advertisement in the Cleveland papers, complimenting them on "the peaceful way in which they laid down their tools." Finding the strike pickets idle, he bought them a couple of dozen baseball bats and gloves and invited them to play ball on vacant lots. For those who preferred bowling, he rented a bowling alley.

This friendliness on Mr. Black's part did what friendliness always does: it begot friendliness. So the strikers borrowed brooms, shovels, and rubbish carts, and began picking up matches, papers, cigarette stubs, and cigar butts around the factory. Imagine it! Imagine strikers tidying up the factory grounds while battling for higher wages and recognition of the union. Such an event had never been heard of before in the long, tempestuous history of American labor wars. That strike ended with a compromise settlement within a week—ended without any ill feeling or rancor.

Daniel Webster, who looked like a god and talked like Jehovah, was one of the most successful advocates who ever pleaded a case; yet he ushered in his most powerful arguments with such friendly remarks as: "It will be for the jury to consider," "This may perhaps be worth thinking of," "Here are some facts that I trust you will not lose sight of," or "You, with your knowledge of human nature, will easily see the significance of these facts." No bulldozing. No high-pressure methods. No attempt to force his opinions on others. Webster used the soft-spoken, quiet, friendly approach, and it helped to make him famous.

You may never be called upon to settle a strike or address a jury, but you may want to get your rent reduced. Will the friendly approach help you then? Let's see.

O. L. Straub, an engineer, wanted to get his rent reduced. And he knew his landlord was hard-boiled. "I wrote to him," Mr. Straub said in a speech before the class, "notifying him that I was vacating my apartment as soon as my lease expired. The truth was, I didn't want to move. I wanted to stay if I could get my rent reduced. But the situation seemed hopeless. Other tenants had tried—and failed. Everyone told me that the landlord was extremely difficult to deal with. But I said to myself, 'I am studying a course in how to deal with people, so I'll try it on him—and see how it works.'"

"He and his secretary came to see me as soon as he got my letter. I met him at the door with a friendly greeting. I fairly bubbled with goodwill and enthusiasm. I didn't begin talking about how high the rent was. I began talking about how much I liked his apartment house. Believe me, I was 'hearty in my approbation and lavish in my praise.' I complimented him on the way he ran the building and told him I really wanted to stay for another year but I couldn't afford it.

"He had evidently never had such a reception from a tenant. He hardly knew what to make of it.

"Then he started to tell me his troubles. Complaining about tenants. One had written him fourteen letters, some of them positively insulting. Another threatened to break his lease unless the landlord kept the man on the floor above from snoring. 'What a relief it is,' he said, 'to have a satisfied tenant like you.' And then, without even asking him to do it, he offered to reduce my rent a little. I wanted more, so I named the figure I could afford to pay, and he accepted without a word.

"As he was leaving, he turned to me and asked, 'What decorating can I do for you?'"

"If I had tried to get the rent reduced by the methods the other tenants were using, I am positive I should have met with the same failure they encountered. It was the friendly, sympathetic, appreciative approach that won."

Dean Woodcock of Pittsburgh, Pennsylvania, is the superintendent of a department of the local electric company. His staff was called upon to repair some equipment on top of a pole. This type of work had formerly been performed by a different department and had only recently been transferred to Woodcock's section. Although his people had been trained in the work, this was the first time they had ever actually been called upon to do it. Everybody in the organization was interested in seeing if and how they could handle it. Mr. Woodcock, several of his subordinate managers, and members of other departments of the utility went to see the operation. Many cars and trucks were there, and a number of people were standing around watching the two lone men on top of the pole.

Glancing around, Woodcock noticed a man up the street getting out of his car with a camera. He began taking pictures of the scene. Utility people are extremely conscious of public relations, and suddenly Woodcock realized what this set-up looked like to the man with the camera—overkill, dozens of people being called out to do a two-person job. He strolled up the street to the photographer.

"I see you're interested in our operation."

"Yes, and my mother will be more than interested. She owns stock in your company. This will be an eye-opener for her. She may even decide her investment was unwise. I've been telling her for years there's a lot of waste motion in companies like yours. This proves it. The newspapers might like these pictures, too."

"It does look like it, doesn't it? I'd think the same thing in your position. But this is a unique situation..." and Dean Woodcock went on to explain how this was the first job of this type for his department and how everybody from executives down was interested. He assured the man that under normal conditions two people could handle the job. The photographer put away his camera, shook Woodcock's hand, and thanked him for taking the time to explain the situation to him.

Dean Woodcock's friendly approach saved his company much embarrassment and bad publicity.

Another member of one of our classes, Gerald H. Winn of Littleton, New Hampshire, reported how by using a friendly approach, he obtained a very satisfactory settlement on a damage claim.

"Early in the spring," he reported, "before the ground had thawed from the winter freezing, there was an unusually heavy rainstorm and the water, which normally would have run off to nearby ditches and storm drains along the road, took a new course onto a building lot where I had just built a new home.

"Not being able to run off, the water pressure built up around the foundation of the house. The water forced itself under the concrete basement floor, causing it to explode, and the basement filled with water. This ruined the furnace and the hot-water heater. The cost to repair this damage was in excess of two thousand dollars. I had no insurance to cover this type of damage.

"However, I soon found out that the owner of the subdivision had neglected to put in a storm drain near the house which could have prevented this problem. I made an appointment to see him. During the twenty-five-mile trip to his office, I carefully reviewed the situation and, remembering the principles I learned in this course, I decided that showing my anger would not serve any worthwhile purpose. When I arrived, I kept very calm and started by talking about his recent vacation to the West Indies; then, when I felt the timing was right, I mentioned the 'little' problem of water damage. He quickly agreed to do his share in helping to correct the problem.

"A few days later he called and said he would pay for the damage and also put in a storm drain to prevent the same thing from happening in the future.

"Even though it was the fault of the owner of the subdivision, if I had not begun in a friendly way, there would have been a great deal of difficulty in getting him to agree to the total liability."

Years ago, when I was a barefoot boy walking through the woods to a country school out in Northwest Missouri, I read a fable about the sun and the wind. They quarreled about which was stronger, and the wind said, "I'll prove I am. See the old man down there with a coat? I bet I can get his coat off him quicker than you can."

So the sun went behind a cloud, and the wind blew until it was almost a tornado, but the harder it blew, the tighter the old man clutched his coat to him.

Finally, the wind calmed down and gave up, and then the sun came out from behind the clouds and smiled kindly on the old man. Presently, he mopped his brow and pulled off his coat. The sun then told the wind that gentleness and friendliness were always stronger than fury and force.

The use of gentleness and friendliness is demonstrated day after day by people who have learned that a drop of honey catches more flies than a gallon of gall. F. Gale Connor of Lutherville, Maryland, proved this when he had to take his four-month-old car to the service department of the car dealer for the third time. He told our class, "It was apparent that talking to, reasoning with or shouting at the service manager was not going to lead to a satisfactory resolution of my problems.

"I walked over to the showroom and asked to see the agency owner, Mr. White. After a short wait, I was ushered into Mr. White's office. I introduced myself and explained to him that I had bought my car from his dealership because of the recommendations of friends who had had previous dealings with him. I was told that his prices were very competitive and his service was outstanding. He smiled with satisfaction as he listened to me. I then explained the problem I was having with the service department. 'I thought you might want to be aware of any situation that might tarnish your fine reputation,' I added. He thanked me for calling this to his attention and assured me that my problem would be taken care of. Not only did he personally get involved, but he also lent me his car to use while mine was being repaired."

Aesop was a Greek slave who lived at the court of Croesus and spun immortal fables six hundred years before Christ. Yet the truths he taught about human nature are just as true in Boston and Birmingham now as they were twenty-six centuries ago in Athens. The sun can make you take off your coat more quickly than the wind; and kindliness, the friendly approach and appreciation can make people change their minds more readily than all the bluster and storming in the world.

Remember what Lincoln said, "A drop of honey catches more flies than a gallon of gall."

⇒ PRINCIPLE 4 ⇐

Begin in a friendly way.

↣ 14 ↢

"THE SECRET OF SOCRATES."

In talking with people, don't begin by discussing the things on which you differ. Begin by emphasizing—and keep on emphasizing—the things on which you agree. Keep emphasizing, if possible, that you are both striving for the same end and that your only difference is one of method and not of purpose.

Get the other person saying "Yes, yes" at the outset. Keep your opponent, if possible, from saying "No." A "No" response, according to Professor Overstreet,* is a most difficult handicap to overcome. When you have said "No," all your pride of personality demands that you remain consistent with yourself. You may later feel that the "No" was ill-advised; nevertheless, there is your precious pride to consider! Once having said a thing, you feel you must stick to it. Hence it is of the very greatest importance that a person be started in the affirmative direction.

* Harry A. Overstreet, *Influencing Human Behavior* (New York: Norton, 1925).

The skillful speaker gets, at the outset, a number of "Yes" responses. This sets the psychological process of the listeners moving in the affirmative direction. It is like the movement of a billiard ball. Propel it in one direction, and it takes some force to deflect it; far more force to send it back in the opposite direction.

The psychological patterns here are quite clear. When a person says "No" and really means it, he or she is doing far more than saying a word of two letters. The entire organism—glandular, nervous, muscular—gathers itself together into a condition of rejection. There is, usually in minute but sometimes in observable degree, a physical withdrawal or readiness for withdrawal. The whole neuromuscular system, in short, sets itself on guard against acceptance. When, to the contrary, a person says "Yes," none of the withdrawal activities takes place. The organism is in a forward-moving, accepting, open attitude.

Hence the more "Yeses" we can, at the very outset, induce, the more likely we are to succeed in capturing the attention for our ultimate proposal.

It is a very simple technique—this "yes" response. And yet, how much it is neglected! It often seems as if people get a sense of their own importance by antagonizing others at the outset.

Get a student to say "No" at the beginning, or a customer, child, husband, or wife, and it takes the wisdom and the patience of angels to transform that bristling negative into an affirmative.

The use of this "yes, yes" technique enabled James Eberson, who was a teller in the Greenwich Savings Bank, in New York City, to secure a prospective customer who might otherwise have been lost.

"This man came in to open an account," said Mr. Eberson, "and I gave him our usual form to fill out. Some of the questions he answered willingly, but there were others he flatly refused to answer.

"Before I began the study of human relations, I would have told this prospective depositor that if he refused to give the bank this information, we would have to refuse to accept this account. I am ashamed that I have been guilty of doing that very thing in the past. Naturally, an ultimatum like that made me feel good. I had shown who was boss, that the bank's rules and regulations couldn't be flouted. But that sort of attitude certainly didn't give a feeling of welcome and importance to the man who had walked in to give us his patronage.

"I resolved this morning to use a little horse sense. I resolved not to talk about what the bank wanted but about what the customer wanted. And above all else, I was determined to get him saying 'yes, yes' from the very start. So I agreed with him. I told him the information he refused to give was not absolutely necessary.

"'However,' I said, 'suppose you have money in this bank at your death. Wouldn't you like to have the bank transfer it to your next of kin, who is entitled to it according to law?'

"'Yes, of course,' he replied.

"'Don't you think,' I continued, 'that it would be a good idea to give us the name of your next of kin so that, in the event of your death, we could carry out your wishes without error or delay?'"

"Again he said, 'Yes.'

"The young man's attitude softened and changed when he realized that we weren't asking for this information for our sake but for his sake. Before leaving the bank, this young man not only gave me complete information about himself but he opened, at my suggestion, a trust account, naming his mother as the beneficiary for his account, and he had gladly answered all the questions concerning his mother also.

"I found that by getting him to say 'yes, yes' from the outset, he forgot the issue at stake and was happy to do all the things I suggested."

Joseph Allison, a sales representative for Westinghouse Electric Company, had this story to tell: "There was a man in my territory that our company was most eager to sell to. My predecessor had called on him for ten years without selling anything. When I took over the territory, I called steadily for three years without getting an order. Finally, after thirteen years of calls and sales talk, we sold him a few motors. If these proved to be all right, an order for several hundred more would follow. Such was my expectation, right? I knew they would be all right. So when I called three weeks later, I was in high spirits.

"The chief engineer greeted me with this shocking announcement: 'Allison, I can't buy the remainder of the motors from you.'

"'Why?' I asked in amazement. 'Why?'

"'Because your motors are too hot. I can't put my hand on them.'"

"I knew it wouldn't do any good to argue. I had tried that sort of thing too long. So I thought of getting the 'yes, yes' response.

"'Well, now look, Mr. Smith,' I said. 'I agree with you a hundred percent; if those motors are running too hot, you ought not to buy any more of them. You must have motors that won't run any hotter than standards set by the National Electrical Manufacturers Association. Isn't that so?'

"He agreed it was. I had gotten my first 'yes.'

"'The Electrical Manufacturers Association regulations say that a properly designed motor may have a temperature of 72 degrees Fahrenheit above room temperature. Is that correct?'

"'Yes,' he agreed. 'That's quite correct. But your motors are much hotter.'

"I didn't argue with him. I merely asked, 'How hot is the mill room?'

"'Oh,' he said, 'about 75 degrees Fahrenheit.'

"'Well,' I replied, 'if the mill room is 75 degrees and you add 72 to that, that makes a total of 147 degrees Fahrenheit. Wouldn't you scald your hand if you held it under a spigot of hot water at a temperature of 147 degrees Fahrenheit?'

"Again he had to say 'yes.'

"'Well,' I suggested, 'wouldn't it be a good idea to keep your hands off those motors?'

"'Well, I guess you're right,' he admitted. We continued to chat for a while. Then he called his secretary and lined up approximately $35,000 worth of business for the ensuing month.

"It took me years and cost me countless thousands of dollars in lost business before I finally learned that it doesn't pay to argue, that it is much more profitable and much more interesting to look at things from the other person's viewpoint and try to get that person saying 'yes, yes.'"

Eddie Snow, who sponsors our courses in Oakland, California, tells how he became a good customer of a shop because the proprietor got him to say "yes, yes." Eddie had become interested in bow hunting and had spent considerable money in purchasing equipment and supplies from a local bow store. When his brother was visiting him he wanted to rent a bow for him from this store. The sales clerk told him they didn't rent bows, so Eddie phoned another bow store. Eddie described what happened:

"A very pleasant gentleman answered the phone. His response to my question for a rental was completely different from the other place. He said he was sorry but they no longer rented bows because they couldn't afford to do so. He then asked me if I had rented before. I replied, 'Yes, several years ago.' He reminded me that I probably paid $25 to $30 for the rental. I said 'yes' again. He then asked if I was the kind of person who liked to save money. Naturally, I answered 'yes.' He went on to explain that they had bow sets with all the necessary equipment on sale for $34.95. I could buy a complete set for only $4.95 more than I could rent one. He explained that is why they had discontinued renting them. Did I think that was reasonable? My 'yes' response led to a purchase of the set, and when I picked it up I purchased several more items at this shop and have since become a regular customer."

Socrates, "the gadfly of Athens," was one of the greatest philosophers the world has ever known. He did something that only a handful of men in all history have been able to do: he sharply changed the whole course of human thought; and now, twenty-four centuries after his death, he is honored as one of the wisest persuaders who ever influenced this wrangling world.

His method? Did he tell people they were wrong? Oh, no, not Socrates. He was far too adroit for that. His whole technique, now called the 'Socratic method,' was based upon getting a "yes, yes" response. He asked questions with which his opponent would have to agree. He kept on winning one admission after another until he had an armful of yeses. He kept on asking questions until finally, almost without realizing it, his opponents found themselves embracing a conclusion they would have bitterly denied a few minutes previously.

The next time we are tempted to tell someone he or she is wrong, let's remember old Socrates and ask a gentle question—a question that will get the "yes, yes" response.

The Chinese have a proverb pregnant with the age-old wisdom of the Orient: "He who treads softly goes far."

They have spent five thousand years studying human nature, those cultured Chinese, and they have garnered a lot of perspicacity: "He who treads softly goes far."

⇒ PRINCIPLE 5 ⇐

Get the other person saying "yes, yes" immediately.

↣ 15 ↢

"THE SAFETY VALVE IN HANDLING COMPLAINTS."

Most people trying to win others to their way of thinking do too much talking themselves. Let the other people talk themselves out. They know more about their business and problems than you do. So ask them questions. Let them tell you a few things.

If you disagree with them you may be tempted to interrupt. But don't. It is dangerous. They won't pay attention to you while they still have a lot of ideas of their own crying for expression. So listen patiently and with an open mind. Be sincere about it. Encourage them to express their ideas fully.

Does this policy pay in business? Let's see. Here is the story of a sales representative who was forced to try it.

One of the largest automobile manufacturers in the United States was negotiating for a year's requirements of upholstery fabrics. Three important manufacturers had worked up fabrics in sample bodies. These had all been inspected by the executives of the motor company, and notice had been sent to each manufacturer saying that, on a certain day, a representative from each supplier would be given an opportunity to make a final plea for the contract.

G.B.R., a representative of one manufacturer, arrived in town with a severe attack of laryngitis. "When it came my turn to meet the executives in conference," Mr. R. said as he related the story before one of my classes, "I had lost my voice. I could hardly whisper. I was ushered into a room and found myself face to face with the textile engineer, the purchasing agent, the director of sales and the president of the company. I stood up and made a valiant effort to speak, but I couldn't do anything more than squeak.

"They were all seated around a table, so I wrote on a pad of paper: 'Gentlemen, I have lost my voice. I am speechless.'

"'I'll do the talking for you,' the president said. He did. He exhibited my samples and praised their good points. A lively discussion arose about the merits of my goods. And the president, since he was talking for me, took the position I would have had during the discussion. My sole participation consisted of smiles, nods and a few gestures.

"As a result of this unique conference, I was awarded the contract, which called for over half a million yards of upholstery fabrics at an aggregate value of $1,600,000—the biggest order I had ever received.

"I know I would have lost the contract if I hadn't lost my voice, because I had the wrong idea about the whole proposition. I discovered, quite by accident, how richly it sometimes pays to let the other person do the talking."

Letting the other person do the talking helps in family situations as well as in business. Barbara Wilson's relationship with her daughter, Laurie, was deteriorating rapidly. Laurie, who had been a quiet, complacent child, had grown into an uncooperative, sometimes belligerent teenager. Mrs. Wilson lectured her, threatened her and punished her, but all to no avail.

"One day," Mrs. Wilson told one of our classes, "I just gave up. Laurie had disobeyed me and had left the house to visit her girl friend before she had completed her chores. When she returned I was about to scream at her for the ten-thousandth time, but I just didn't have the strength to do it. I just looked at her and said sadly, 'Why, Laurie, Why?'

"Laurie noted my condition and in a calm voice asked, 'Do you really want to know?' I nodded and Laurie told me, first hesitantly, and then it all flowed out. I had never listened to her. I was always telling her to do this or that. When she wanted to tell me her thoughts, feelings, ideas, I interrupted with more orders. I began to realize that she needed me—not as a bossy mother, but as a confidante, an outlet for all her confusion about growing up. And all I had been doing was talking when I should have been listening. I never heard of her.

"From that time on I let her do all the talking she wanted. She tells me what is on her mind, and our relationship has improved immeasurably. She is again a cooperative person."

A large advertisement appeared on the financial page of a New York newspaper calling for a person with unusual ability and experience. Charles T. Cubellis answered the advertisement, sending his reply to a box number. A few days later, he was invited by letter to call for an interview. Before he called, he spent hours in Wall Street finding out everything possible about the person who had founded the business. During the interview, he remarked, "I should be mighty proud to be associated with an organization with a record like yours. I understand you started twenty-eight years ago with nothing but desk room and one stenographer. Is that true?"

Almost every successful person likes to reminisce about his early struggles. This man was no exception. He talked for a long time about how he had started with $450 in cash and an original idea. He told how he had fought against discouragement and battled against ridicule, working Sundays and holidays, twelve to sixteen hours a day; how he had finally won against all odds until now the most important executives on Wall Street were coming to him for information and guidance. He was proud of such a record. He had a right to be, and he had a splendid time telling about it. Finally, he questioned Mr. Cubellis briefly about his experience, then called in one of his vice presidents and said, "I think this is the person we are looking for."

Mr. Cubellis had taken the trouble to find out about the accomplishments of his prospective employer. He showed an interest in the other person and his problems. He encouraged the other person to do most of the talking—and made a favorable impression.

Roy G. Bradley of Sacramento, California, had the opposite problem. He listened as a good prospect for a sales position talked himself into a job with Bradley's firm. Roy reported:

"Being a small brokerage firm, we had no fringe benefits, such as hospitalization, medical insurance and pensions. Every representative is an independent agent. We don't even provide leads for prospects, as we cannot advertise for them as our larger competitors do.

"Richard Pryor had the type of experience we wanted for this position, and he was interviewed first by my assistant, who told him about all the negatives related to this job. He seemed slightly discouraged when he came into my office. I mentioned the one benefit of being associated with my firm, that of being an independent contractor and therefore virtually being self-employed.

"As he talked about these advantages to me, he talked himself out of each negative thought he had when he came in for the interview. Several times it seemed as though he was half-talking to himself as he was thinking through each thought. At times I was tempted to add to his thoughts; however, as the interview came to a close I felt he had convinced himself, very much on his own, that he would like to work for my firm.

"Because I had been a good listener and let Dick do most of the talking, he was able to weigh both sides fairly in his mind, and he came to the positive conclusion, which was a challenge he created for himself. We hired him and he has been an outstanding representative for our firm."

Even our friends would much rather talk to us about their achievements than listen to us boast about ours. La Rochefoucauld, the French philosopher, said, "If you want enemies, excel your friends; but if you want friends, let your friends excel you."

Why is that true? Because when our friends excel us, they feel important; but when we excel them, they—or at least some of them—will feel inferior and envious.

By far the best-liked placement counselor in the Midtown Personnel Agency in New York City was Henrietta G. It hadn't always been that way. During the first few months of her association with the agency, Henrietta didn't have a single friend among her colleagues. Why? Because every day she would brag about the placements she had made, the new accounts she had opened, and anything else she had accomplished.

"I was good at my work and proud of it," Henrietta told one of our classes. "But instead of my colleagues sharing my triumphs, they seemed to resent them. I wanted to be liked by these people. I really wanted them to be my friends. After listening to some of the suggestions made in this course, I started to talk about myself less and listen more to my associates. They also had things to boast about and were more excited about telling me about their accomplishments than about listening to my boasting. Now, when we have some time to chat, I ask them to share their joys with me, and I only mention my achievements when they ask."

⇒ PRINCIPLE 6 ⇐

Let the other person do a great deal of the talking.

↣ 16 ↢

"HOW TO GET COOPERATION."

Don't you have much more faith in ideas that you discover for yourself than in ideas that are handed to you on a silver platter? If so, isn't it bad judgment to try to ram your opinions down the throats of other people? Isn't it wiser to make suggestions—and let the other person think out the conclusion?

Adolph Seltz of Philadelphia, sales manager in an automobile showroom and a student in one of my courses, suddenly found himself confronted with the necessity of injecting enthusiasm into a discouraged and disorganized group of automobile salespeople. Calling a sales meeting, he urged his people to tell him exactly what they expected from him. As they talked, he wrote their ideas on the blackboard. He then said, "I'll give you all these qualities you expect from me. Now I want you to tell me what I have a right to expect from you."

The replies came quick and fast: loyalty, honesty, initiative, optimism, teamwork, eight hours a day of enthusiastic work. The meeting ended with a new courage, a new inspiration—one salesperson volunteered to work fourteen hours a day—and Mr. Seltz reported to me that the increase of sales was phenomenal.

"The people had made a sort of moral bargain with me," said Mr. Seltz, "and as long as I lived up to my part in it, they were determined to live up to theirs. Consulting them about their wishes and desires was just the shot in the arm they needed."

No one likes to feel that he or she is being sold something or told to do a thing. We much prefer to feel that we are buying of our own accord or acting on our own ideas. We like to be consulted about our wishes, our wants, our thoughts.

Take the case of Eugene Wesson. He lost countless thousands of dollars in commissions before he learned this truth. Mr. Wesson sold sketches for a studio that created designs for stylists and textile manufacturers. Mr. Wesson had called on one of the leading stylists in New York once a week, every week for three years. "He never refused to see me," said Mr. Wesson, "but he never bought. He always looked over my sketches very carefully and then said, 'No, Wesson, I guess we don't get any today.'"

After 150 failures, Wesson realized he must be in a mental rut, so he resolved to devote one evening a week to the study of influencing human behavior, to help him develop new ideas and generate new enthusiasm.

He decided on this new approach. With half a dozen unfinished artists' sketches under his arm, he rushed over to the buyer's office. "I want you to do me a little favor, if you will," he said. "Here are some uncompleted sketches. Won't you please tell me how we could finish them up in such a way that you could use them?"

The buyer looked at the sketches for a while without uttering a word. Finally he said, "Leave these with me for a few days, Wesson, and then come back and see me."

Wesson returned three days later, got his suggestions, took the sketches back to the studio and had them finished according to the buyer's ideas. The result? All accepted.

After that, this buyer ordered scores of other sketches from Wesson, all drawn according to the buyer's ideas. "I realized why I had failed for years to sell him," said Mr. Wesson. "I had urged him to buy what I thought he ought to have. Then I changed my approach completely. I urged him to give me his ideas. This made him feel that he was creating the designs. And he was. I didn't have to sell him. He bought."

Letting the other person feel that the idea is his or hers not only works in business and politics, it works in family life as well. Paul M. Davis of Tulsa, Oklahoma, told his class how he applied this principle:

"My family and I enjoyed one of the most interesting sightseeing vacation trips we have ever taken. I had long dreamed of visiting such historic sites as the Civil War battlefield in Gettysburg, Independence Hall in Philadelphia, and our nation's capital. Valley Forge, Jamestown and the restored colonial village of Williamsburg were high on the list of things I wanted to see.

"In March my wife, Nancy, mentioned that she had ideas for our summer vacation which included a tour of the western states, visiting points of interest in New Mexico, Arizona, California and Nevada. She had wanted to make this trip for several years. But we obviously couldn't make both trips.

"Our daughter, Anne, had just completed a course in U.S. history in junior high school and had become very interested in the events that had shaped our country's growth. I asked her how she would like to visit the places she had learned about on our next vacation. She said she would love to.

"Two evenings later as we sat around the dinner table, Nancy announced that if we all agreed, the summer's vacation would be to the eastern states, that it would be a great trip for Anne and thrilling for all of us. We all concurred."

This same psychology was used by an X-ray manufacturer to sell his equipment to one of the largest hospitals in Brooklyn. This hospital was building an addition and preparing to equip it with the finest X-ray department in America. Dr. L., who was in charge of the X-ray department, was overwhelmed with sales representatives, each caroling the praises of his own company's equipment.

One manufacturer, however, was more skillful. He knew far more about handling human nature than the others did. He wrote a letter something like this:

"Our factory has recently completed a new line of X-ray equipment. The first shipment of these machines has just arrived at our office. They are not perfect. We know that, and we want to improve them. So we should be deeply obligated to you if you could find time to look them over and give us your ideas about how they can be made more serviceable to your profession. Knowing how occupied you are, I shall be glad to send my car for you at any hour you specify."

"I was surprised to get that letter," Dr. L. said as he related the incident before the class. "I was both surprised and complimented. I had never had an X-ray manufacturer seeking my advice before. It made me feel important. I was busy every night that week, but I canceled a dinner appointment in order to look over the equipment. The more I studied it, the more I discovered for myself how much I liked it.

"Nobody had tried to sell it to me. I felt that the idea of buying that equipment for the hospital was my own. I sold myself on its superior qualities and ordered it installed."

Ralph Waldo Emerson in his essay "Self-Reliance" stated, "In every work of genius we recognize our own rejected thoughts; they come back to us with a certain alienated majesty."

Colonel Edward M. House wielded an enormous influence in national and international affairs while Woodrow Wilson occupied the White House. Wilson leaned upon Colonel House for secret counsel and advice more than he did upon even members of his own cabinet.

What method did the Colonel use in influencing the President? Fortunately, we know, for House himself revealed it to Arthur D. Howden Smith, and Smith quoted House in an article in The Saturday Evening Post:

"'After I got to know the President,' House said, 'I learned the best way to convert him to an idea was to plant it in his mind casually, but so as to interest him in it—so as to get him thinking about it on his own account. The first time this worked it was an accident. I had been visiting him at the White House and urged a policy on him which he appeared to disapprove of. But several days later, at the dinner table, I was amazed to hear him trot out my suggestion as his own.'"

Did House interrupt him and say, "That's not your idea. That's mine"? Oh, no. Not House. He was too adroit for that. He didn't care about credit. He wanted results. So he let Wilson continue to feel that the idea was his. House did even more than that. He gave Wilson public credit for these ideas.

Let's remember that everyone we come in contact with is just as human as Woodrow Wilson. So let's use Colonel House's technique.

A man up in the beautiful Canadian province of New Brunswick used this technique on me and won my patronage. I was planning at the time to do some fishing and canoeing in New Brunswick. So I wrote to the tourist bureau for information. Evidently my name and address were put on a mailing list, for I was immediately overwhelmed with scores of letters and booklets and printed testimonials from camps and guides. I was bewildered. I didn't know which to choose. Then one camp owner did a clever thing. He sent me the names and telephone numbers of several New York people who had stayed at his camp and he invited me to telephone them and discover for myself what he had to offer.

I found to my surprise that I knew one of the men on his list. I telephoned him, found out what his experience had been, and then wired the camp the date of my arrival.

The others had been trying to sell me on their service, but one let me sell myself. That organization won. Twenty-five centuries ago, Lao-tse, a Chinese sage, said some things that readers of this book might use today:

"The reason why rivers and seas receive the homage of a hundred mountain streams is that they keep below them. Thus they are able to reign over all the mountain streams. So the sage, wishing to be above men, putteth himself below them; wishing to be before them, he putteth himself behind them. Thus, though his place is above men, they do not feel his weight; though his place be before them, they do not count it an injury."

⇒ PRINCIPLE 7 ⇐

Let the other person feel that the idea is his or hers.

↣ 17 ↢

"A FORMULA THAT WILL WORK WONDERS FOR YOU."

Remember that other people may be totally wrong. But they don't think so. Don't condemn them. Any fool can do that. Try to understand them. Only wise, tolerant, exceptional people even try to do that.

There is a reason why the other man thinks and acts as he does. Ferret out that reason—and you have the key to his actions, perhaps to his personality. Try honestly to put yourself in his place.

If you say to yourself, "How would I feel, how would I react if I were in his shoes?" you will save yourself time and irritation, for "by becoming interested in the cause, we are less likely to dislike the effect." And, in addition, you will sharply increase your skill in human relationships.

"Stop a minute," says Kenneth M. Goode in his book *How to Turn People Into Gold*, "stop a minute to contrast your keen interest in your own affairs with your mild concern about anything else. Realize then, that everybody else in the world feels exactly the same way! Then, along with Lincoln and Roosevelt, you will have grasped the only solid foundation for interpersonal relationships; namely, that success in dealing with people depends on a sympathetic grasp of the other person's viewpoint."

Sam Douglas of Hempstead, New York, used to tell his wife that she spent too much time working on their lawn, pulling weeds, fertilizing, and cutting the grass twice a week when the lawn didn't look any better than it had when they moved into their home four years earlier. Naturally, she was distressed by his remarks, and each time he made such remarks the balance of the evening was ruined.

After taking our course, Mr. Douglas realized how foolish he had been all those years. It never occurred to him that she enjoyed doing that work and she might really appreciate a compliment on her diligence.

One evening after dinner, his wife said she wanted to pull some weeds and invited him to keep her company. He first declined, but then thought better of it and went out after her and began to help her pull weeds. She was visibly pleased, and together they spent an hour in hard work and pleasant conversation.

After that he often helped her with the gardening and complimented her on how fine the lawn looked, what a fantastic job she was doing with a yard where the soil was like concrete. Result: a happier life for both because he had learned to look at things from her point of view—even if the subject was only weeds.

In his book *Getting Through to People*, Dr. Gerald S. Nirenberg commented, "Cooperativeness in conversation is achieved when you show that you consider the other person's ideas and feelings as important as your own. Starting your conversation by giving the other person the purpose or direction of your conversation, governing what you say by what you would want to hear if you were the listener, and accepting his or her viewpoint will encourage the listener to have an open mind to your ideas." *

* Dr Gerald S. Nirenberg, Getting Through to People (Englewood Cliffs, N.J.: Prentice-Hall, 1963), p. 31.

I have always enjoyed walking and riding in a park near my home. Like the Druids of ancient Gaul, I all but worship an oak tree, so I was distressed season after season to see the young trees and shrubs killed off by needless fires. These fires weren't caused by careless smokers. They were almost all caused by youngsters who went out to the park to go native and cook a frankfurter or an egg under the trees. Sometimes, these fires raged so fiercely that the fire department had to be called out to fight the conflagration.

There was a sign on the edge of the park saying that anyone who started a fire was liable to fine and imprisonment, but the sign stood in an unfrequented part of the park, and few of the culprits ever saw it. A mounted policeman was supposed to look after the park; but he didn't take his duties too seriously, and the fires continued to spread season after season. On one occasion, I rushed up to a policeman and told him about a fire spreading rapidly through the park and wanted him to notify the fire department, and he nonchalantly replied that it was none of his business because it wasn't in his precinct! I was desperate, so after that when I went riding, I acted as a self-appointed committee of one to protect the public domain. In the beginning, I am afraid I didn't even attempt to see the other people's point of view. When I saw a fire blazing under the trees, I was so unhappy about it, so eager to do the right thing, that I did the wrong thing. I would ride up to the boys, warn them that they could be jailed for starting a fire, order with a tone of authority that it be put out; and, if they refused, I would threaten to have them arrested. I was merely unloading my feelings without thinking of their point of view.

The result? They obeyed...obeyed sullenly and with resentment. After I rode on over the hill, they probably rebuilt the fire and longed to burn up the whole park.

With the passing of the years, I acquired a trifle more knowledge of human relations, a little more tact, a somewhat greater tendency to see things from the other person's standpoint. Then, instead of giving orders, I would ride up to a blazing fire and begin something like this:

"Having a good time, boys? What are you going to cook for supper? I loved to build fires myself when I was a boy, and I still love to. But you know they are very dangerous here in the park. I know you boys don't mean to do any harm, but other boys aren't so careful. They come along and see that you have built a fire; so they build one and don't put it out when they go home and it spreads among the dry leaves and kills the trees. We won't have any trees here at all if we aren't more careful. You could be put in jail for building this fire. But I don't want to be bossy and interfere with your pleasure. I like to see you enjoy yourselves; but won't you please rake all the leaves away from the fire right now, and you'll be careful to cover it with dirt, a lot of dirt, before you leave, won't you? And the next time you want to have some fun, won't you please build your fire over the hill there in the sandpit? It can't do any harm there. Thanks so much, boys. Have a good time."

What a difference that kind of talk made! It made the boys want to cooperate. No sullenness, no resentment. They hadn't been forced to obey orders. They had saved their faces. They felt better and I felt better because I had handled the situation with consideration for their point of view.

Seeing things through another person's eyes may ease tensions when personal problems become overwhelming. Elizabeth Novak of New South Wales, Australia, was six weeks late with her car payment. "On a Friday," she reported, "I received a nasty phone call from the man who was handling my account informing me that if I did not come up with $122 by Monday morning I could anticipate further action from the company. I had no way of raising the money over the weekend, so when I received his phone call first thing on Monday morning I expected the worst. Instead of becoming upset I looked at the situation from his point of view. I apologized most sincerely for causing him so much inconvenience and remarked that I must be his most troublesome customer as this was not the first time I was behind in my payments. His tone of voice changed immediately, and he reassured me that I was far from being one of his really troublesome customers. He went on to tell me several examples of how rude his customers sometimes were, how they lied to him and often tried to avoid talking to him at all. I said nothing. I listened and let him pour out his troubles to me. Then, without any suggestion from me, he said it did not matter if I couldn't pay all the money immediately. It would be all right if I paid him $20 by the end of the month and made up the balance whenever it was convenient for me to do so."

Tomorrow, before asking anyone to put out a fire or buy your product or contribute to your favorite charity, why not pause and close your eyes and try to think the whole thing through from another person's point of view? Ask yourself: "Why should he or she want to do it?" True, this will take time, but it will avoid making enemies and will get better results, and with less friction and less shoe leather.

"I would rather walk the sidewalk in front of a person's office for two hours before an interview," said Dean Donham of the Harvard Business School, "than step into that office without a perfectly clear idea of what I was going to say and what that person—from my knowledge of his or her interests and motives—was likely to answer."

That is so important that I am going to repeat it in italics for the sake of emphasis.

I would rather walk the sidewalk in front of a person's office for two hours before an interview than step into that office without a perfectly clear idea of what I was going to say and what that person—from my knowledge of his or her interests and motives—was likely to answer.

If, as a result of reading this book, you get only one thing—an increased tendency to think always in terms of the other person's point of view, and see things from that person's angle as well as your own - if you get only that one thing from this book, it may easily prove to be one of the stepping stones of your career.

⇒ PRINCIPLE 8 ⇐

Try honestly to see things from the other person's point of view.

↣ 18 ↢

"WHAT EVERYBODY WANTS."

Wouldn't you like to have a magic phrase that would stop arguments, eliminate ill feeling, create good will, and make the other person listen attentively?

Yes? All right. Here it is: "I don't blame you one iota for feeling as you do. If I were you I would undoubtedly feel just as you do."

An answer like that will soften the most cantankerous old cuss alive. And you can say that and be 100 percent sincere, because if you were the other person you, of course, would feel just as he does. Take Al Capone, for example. Suppose you had inherited the same body and temperament and mind that Al Capone had. Suppose you had had his environment and experiences. You would then be precisely what he was, and where he was. For it is those things—and only those things—that made him what he was. The only reason, for example, that you are not a rattlesnake is that your mother and father weren't rattlesnakes.

You deserve very little credit for being what you are—and remember, the people who come to you irritated, bigoted, unreasoning, deserve very little discredit for being what they are. Feel sorry for the poor devils. Pity them. Sympathize with them. Say to yourself, "There, but for the grace of God, go I."

Three-fourths of the people you will ever meet are hungering and thirsting for sympathy. Give it to them, and they will love you.

I once gave a broadcast about the author of Little Women, Louisa May Alcott. Naturally, I knew she had lived and written her immortal books in Concord, Massachusetts. But, without thinking what I was saying, I spoke of visiting her old home in Concord, New Hampshire. If I had said New Hampshire only once, it might have been forgiven. But, alas and alack! I said it twice. I was deluged with letters and telegrams, stinging messages that swirled around my defenseless head like a swarm of hornets. Many were indignant. A few insults. One Colonial Dame, who had been reared in Concord, Massachusetts, and who was then living in Philadelphia, vented her scorching wrath upon me. She couldn't have been much more bitter if I had accused Miss Alcott of being a cannibal from New Guinea. As I read the letter, I said to myself, "Thank God, I am not married to that woman." I felt like writing and telling her that although I had made a mistake in geography, she had made a far greater mistake in common courtesy. That was to be just my opening sentence. Then I was going to roll up my sleeves and tell her what I really thought. But I didn't. I controlled myself. I realized that any hot-headed fool could do that, and that most fools would do just that.

I wanted to be above fools. So I resolved to try to turn her hostility into friendliness. It would be a challenge, a sort of game I could play. I said to myself, "After all, if I were her, I would probably feel just as she does." So, I am determined to sympathize with her viewpoint. The next time I was in Philadelphia, I called her on the telephone. The conversation went something like this:

ME: Mrs. So-and-So, you wrote me a letter a few weeks ago, and I want to thank you for it.

SHE: (in incisive, cultured, well-bred tones): To whom have I the honor of speaking?

ME: I am a stranger to you. My name is Dale Carnegie. You listened to a broadcast I gave about Louisa May Alcott a few Sundays ago, and I made the unforgivable blunder of saying that she had lived in Concord, New Hampshire. It was a stupid blunder, and I want to apologize for it. It was so nice of you to take the time to write to me.

SHE: I am sorry, Mr. Carnegie, that I wrote as I did. I lost my temper. I must apologize.

ME: No! No! You are not the one to apologize; I am. Any school child would have known better than to have said what I said. I apologized over the air the following Sunday, and I want to apologize to you personally now.

SHE: I was born in Concord, Massachusetts. My family has been prominent in Massachusetts affairs for two centuries, and I am very proud of my native state. I was really quite distressed to hear you say that Miss Alcott had lived in New Hampshire. But I am really ashamed of that letter.

ME: I assure you that you were not one-tenth as distressed as I am. My error didn't hurt Massachusetts, but it did hurt me. It is so seldom that people of your standing and culture take the time to write to people who speak on the radio, and I do hope you will write to me again if you detect an error in my talks.

SHE: You know, I really like very much the way you have accepted my criticism. You must be a very nice person. I would like to know you better.

So, because I had apologized and sympathized with her point of view, she began apologizing and sympathizing with my point of view. I had the satisfaction of controlling my temper, the satisfaction of returning kindness for an insult. I got infinitely more real fun out of making her like me than I could ever have gotten out of telling her to go and take a jump in the Schuylkill River.

Every man who occupies the White House is faced almost daily with thorny problems in human relations. President Taft was no exception, and he learned from experience the enormous chemical value of sympathy in neutralizing the acid of hard feelings. In his book Ethics in Service, Taft gives rather an amusing illustration of how he softened the ire of a disappointed and ambitious mother.

"A lady in Washington," wrote Taft, "whose husband had some political influence, came and labored with me for six weeks or more to appoint her son to a position. She secured the aid of Senators and Congressmen in formidable numbers and came with them to see that they spoke with emphasis. The place was one requiring technical qualification, and following the recommendation of the head of the Bureau, I appointed somebody else. I then received a letter from the mother, saying that I was most ungrateful, since I declined to make her a happy woman as I could have done by a turn of my hand. She complained further that she had labored with her state delegation and got all the votes for an administration bill in which I was especially interested and this was the way I had rewarded her.

"When you get a letter like that, the first thing you do is to think how you can be severe with a person who has committed an impropriety, or even been a little impertinent. Then you may compose an answer. Then if you are wise, you will put the letter in a drawer and lock the drawer. Take it out in the course of two days - such communications will always bear two days' delay in answering, and when you take it out after that interval, you will not send it. That is just the course I took. After that, I sat down and wrote her just as polite a letter as I could, telling her I realized a mother's disappointment under such circumstances, but that really the appointment was not left to my mere personal preference, that I had to select a man with technical qualifications, and had, therefore, to follow the recommendations of the head of the Bureau. I expressed the hope that her son would go on to accomplish what she had hoped for him in the position which he then had. That mollified her and she wrote me a note saying she was sorry she had written as she had.

"But the appointment I sent in was not confirmed at once, and after an interval I received a letter which purported to come from her husband, though it was in the same handwriting as all the others. I was therein advised that, due to the nervous prostration that had followed her disappointment in this case, she had to take to her bed and had developed a most serious case of cancer of the stomach. Would I not restore her to health by withdrawing the first name and replacing it with her son's? I had to write another letter, this one to the husband, to say that I hoped the diagnosis would prove to be inaccurate, that I sympathized with him in the sorrow he must have in the serious illness of his wife, but that it was impossible to withdraw the name sent in. The man whom I appointed was confirmed, and within two days after I received that letter, we gave a musical at the White House. The first two people to greet Mrs. Taft and me were this husband and wife, though the wife had so recently been in articulo mortis."

Jay Mangum represented an elevator-escalator maintenance company in Tulsa, Oklahoma, which had the maintenance contract for the escalators in one of Tulsa's leading hotels. The hotel manager did not want to shut down the escalator for more than two hours at a time because he did not want to inconvenience the hotel's guests. The repair that had to be made would take at least eight hours, and his company did not always have a specially qualified mechanic available at the convenience of the hotel.

When Mr. Mangum was able to schedule a top-flight mechanic for this job, he telephoned the hotel manager and instead of arguing with him to give him the necessary time, he said, "Rick, I know your hotel is quite busy and you would like to keep the escalator shutdown time to a minimum. I understand your concern about this, and we want to do everything possible to accommodate you. However, our diagnosis of the situation shows that if we do not do a complete job now, your escalator may suffer more serious damage and that would cause a much longer shutdown. I know you would not want to inconvenience your guests for several days."

The manager had to agree that an eight-hour shutdown was more desirable than several days. By sympathizing with the manager's desire to keep his patrons happy, Mr. Mangum was able to win the hotel manager to his way of thinking easily and without rancor.

Joyce Norris, a piano teacher in St. Louis, Missouri, told of how she had handled a problem piano teachers often have with teenage girls. Babette had exceptionally long fingernails. This is a serious handicap to anyone who wants to develop proper piano-playing habits.

Mrs. Norris reported: "I knew her long fingernails would be a barrier for her in her desire to play well. During our discussions prior to her starting her lessons with me, I did not mention anything to her about her nails. I didn't want to discourage her from taking lessons, and I also knew she would not want to lose that which she took so much pride in and such great care to make attractive.

"After her first lesson, when I felt the time was right, I said, 'Babette, you have attractive hands and beautiful fingernails. If you want to play the piano as well as you are capable of and as well as you would like to, you would be surprised how much quicker and easier it would be for you, if you would trim your nails shorter. Just think about it, okay?' She made a face which was definitely negative. I also talked to her mother about this situation, again mentioning how lovely her nails were. Another negative reaction. It was obvious that Babette's beautifully manicured nails were important to her.

"The following week Babette returned for her second lesson. Much to my surprise, the fingernails had been trimmed. I complimented her and praised her for making such a sacrifice. I also thanked her mother for influencing Babette to cut her nails. Her reply was 'Oh, I had nothing to do with it. Babette decided to do it on her own, and this is the first time she has ever trimmed her nails for anyone.'"

Did Mrs. Norris threaten Babette? Did she say she would refuse to teach a student with long fingernails? No, she did not. She let Babette know that her fingernails were a thing of beauty and it would be a sacrifice to cut them. She implied, "I sympathize with you—I know it won't be easy, but it will pay off in your better musical development."

Sol Hurok was probably America's number one impresario. For almost half a century he handled artists—such world-famous artists as Chaliapin, Isadora Duncan, and Pavlova. Mr. Hurok told me that one of the first lessons he had learned in dealing with his temperamental stars was the necessity for sympathy, sympathy and more sympathy with their idiosyncrasies.

For three years, he was impresario for Feodor Chaliapin—one of the greatest bassos who ever thrilled the ritzy box-holders at the Metropolitan, yet Chaliapin was a constant problem. He carried on like a spoiled child. To put it in Mr. Hurok's own inimitable phrase: "He was a hell of a fellow in every way."

For example, Chaliapin would call up Mr. Hurok about noon of the day he was going to sing and say, "Sol, I feel terrible. My throat is like a raw hamburger. It is impossible for me to sing tonight." Did Mr. Hurok argue with him? Oh, no. He knew that an entrepreneur couldn't handle artists that way. So he would rush over to Chaliapin's hotel, dripping with sympathy. "What a pity," he would mourn. "What a pity! My poor fellow. Of course, you cannot sing. I will cancel the engagement at once. It will only cost you a couple of thousand dollars, but that is nothing in comparison to your reputation."

Then Chaliapin would sigh and say, "Perhaps you had better come over later in the day. Come at five and see how I feel then."

At five o'clock, Mr. Hurok would again rush to his hotel, dripping with sympathy. Again he would insist on canceling the engagement and again Chaliapin would sigh and say, "Well, maybe you had better come to see me later. I may be better then."

At seven-thirty the great basso would consent to sing, only with the understanding that Mr. Hurok would walk out on the stage of the Metropolitan and announce that Chaliapin had a very bad cold and was not in good voice. Mr. Hurok would lie and say he would do it, for he knew that was the only way to get the basso out on the stage.

Dr. Arthur I. Gates said in his splendid book Educational Psychology: "Sympathy the human species universally craves. The child eagerly displays his injury; or even inflicts a cut or bruise in order to reap abundant sympathy. For the same purpose adults...show their bruises, relate their accidents, illness, especially details of surgical operations. 'Self-pity' for misfortunes real or imaginary is in some measure, practically a universal practice."

So, if you want to win people to your way of thinking, put it into practice...

⇒ PRINCIPLE 9 ⇐

Be sympathetic with the other person's ideas and desires.

↣ 19 ↢

"AN APPEAL THAT EVERYBODY LIKES."

I was reared on the edge of the Jesse James country out in Missouri, and I visited the James farm at Kearney, Missouri, where the son of Jesse James was then living.

His wife told me stories of how Jesse robbed trains and held up banks and then gave money to the neighboring farmers to pay off their mortgages.

Jesse James probably regarded himself as an idealist at heart, just as Dutch Schultz, "Two Gun" Crowley, Al Capone and many other organized crime "godfathers" did generations later. The fact is that all people you meet have a high regard for themselves and like to be fine and unselfish in their own estimation.

J. Pierpont Morgan observed, in one of his analytical interludes, that a person usually has two reasons for doing a thing: one that sounds good and a real one.

The person himself will think of the real reason. You don't need to emphasize that. But all of us, being idealists at heart, like to think of motives that sound good. So, in order to change people, appeal to the nobler motives.

Is that too idealistic to work in business? Let's see. Let's take the case of Hamilton J. Farrell of the Farrell-Mitchell Company of Glenolden, Pennsylvania. Mr. Farrell had a disgruntled tenant who threatened to move. The tenant's lease still had four months to run; nevertheless, he served notice that he was vacating immediately, regardless of the lease.

"These people had lived in my house all winter—the most expensive part of the year," Mr. Farrell said as he told the story to the class, "and I knew it would be difficult to rent the apartment again before fall. I could see all that rent income going over the hill and believe me, I saw red.

"Now, ordinarily, I would have waded into that tenant and advised him to read his lease again. I would have pointed out that if he moved, the full balance of his rent would fall due at once—and that I could, and would, move to collect.

"However, instead of flying off the handle and making a scene, I decided to try other tactics. So I started like this: 'Mr. Doe,' I said, 'I have listened to your story, and I still don't believe you intend to move. Years in the renting business have taught me something about human nature, and I sized you up in the first place as being a man of your word. In fact, I'm so sure of it that I'm willing to take a gamble.

"'Now, here's my proposition. Lay your decision on the table for a few days and think it over. If you come back to me between now and the first of the month, when your rent is due, and tell me you still intend to move, I give you my word I will accept your decision as final. I will privilege you to move and admit to myself I've been wrong in my judgment. But I still believe you're a man of your word and will live up to your contract. For after all, we are either men or monkeys—and the choice usually lies with ourselves!'

"Well, when the new month came around, this gentleman came to see me and paid his rent in person. He and his wife had talked it over, he said—and decided to stay. They had concluded that the only honorable thing to do was to live up to their lease."

When the late Lord Northcliffe found a newspaper using a picture of him which he didn't want published, he wrote the editor a letter. But did he say, "Please do not publish that picture of me any more; I don't like it"? No, he appealed to a nobler motive. He appealed to the respect and love that all of us have for motherhood. He wrote, "Please do not publish that picture of me any more. My mother doesn't like it."

When John D. Rockefeller, Jr., wished to stop newspaper photographers from snapping pictures of his children, he too appealed to the nobler motives. He didn't say: "I don't want their pictures published." No, he appealed to the desire, deep in all of us, to refrain from harming children. He said: "You know how it is, boys. You've got children yourselves, some of you. And you know it's not good for youngsters to get too much publicity."

When Cyrus H. K. Curtis, the poor boy from Maine, was starting on his meteoric career, which was destined to make him millions as owner of The Saturday Evening Post and the Ladies' Home Journal, he couldn't afford to pay his contributors the prices that other magazines paid. He couldn't afford to hire first-class authors to write for money alone. So he appealed to their nobler motives. For example, he persuaded even Louisa May Alcott, the immortal author of Little Women, to write for him when she was at the flood tide of her fame; and he did it by offering to send a check for a hundred dollars, not to her, but to her favorite charity.

Right here the skeptic may say: "Oh, that stuff is all right for Northcliffe and Rockefeller or a sentimental novelist. But, I'd like to see you make it work with the tough babies I have to collect bills from!"

You may be right. Nothing will work in all cases—and nothing will work with all people. If you are satisfied with the results you are now getting, why change? If you are not satisfied, why not experiment?

At any rate, I think you will enjoy reading this true story told by James L. Thomas, a former student of mine:

Six customers of a certain automobile company refused to pay their bills for servicing. None of the customers protested the entire bill, but each claimed that some one charge was wrong. In each case, the customer had signed for the work done, so the company knew it was right—and said so. That was the first mistake.

Here are the steps the men in the credit department took to collect these overdue bills. Do you suppose they succeeded?

1. They called on each customer and told him bluntly that they had come to collect a bill that was long past due.

2. They made it very plain that the company was absolutely and unconditionally right; therefore he, the customer, was absolutely and unconditionally wrong.

3. They intimated that they, the company, knew more about automobiles than he could ever hope to know. So what was the argument about?

4. Result: They argued.

Did any of these methods reconcile the customer and settle the account? You can answer that one yourself.

At this stage of affairs, the credit manager was about to open fire with a battery of legal talent, when fortunately the matter came to the attention of the general manager. The manager investigated these defaulting clients and discovered that they all had the reputation of paying their bills promptly. Something was wrong here—something was drastically wrong about the method of collection. So he called in James L. Thomas and told him to collect these "uncollectible" accounts.

Here, in his words, are the steps Mr. Thomas took:

1. My visit to each customer was likewise to collect a bill long past due—a bill that we knew was absolutely right. But I didn't say a word about that. I explained I had called to find out what it was the company had done, or failed to do.

2. I made it clear that, until I had heard the customer's story, I had no opinion to offer. I told him the company made no claims to being infallible.

3. I told him I was interested only in his car, and that he knew more about his car than anyone else in the world; that he was the authority on the subject.

4. I let him talk, and I listened to him with all the interest and sympathy that he wanted—and had expected.

5. Finally, when the customer was in a reasonable mood, I put the whole thing up to his sense of fair play. I appealed to the nobler motives. "First," I said, "I want you to know I also feel this matter has been badly

mishandled. You've been inconvenienced and annoyed and irritated by one of our representatives. That should never have happened. I'm sorry and, as a representative of the company, I apologize. As I sat here and listened to your side of the story, I could not help being impressed by your fairness and patience. And now, because you are fair-minded and patient, I am going to ask you to do something for me. It's something that you can do better than anyone else, something you know more about than anyone else. Here is your bill; I know it is safe for me to ask you to adjust it, just as you would do if you were the president of my company. I am going to leave it all up to you. Whatever you say goes."

Did he adjust the bill? He certainly did, and got quite a kick out of it. The bills ranged from $150 to $400—but did the customer give himself the best of it? Yes, one of them did! One of them refused to pay a penny of the disputed charge; but the other five all gave the company the best of it! And here's the cream of the whole thing: we delivered new cars to all six of these customers within the next two years!

"Experience has taught me," says Mr. Thomas, "that when no information can be secured about the customer, the only sound basis on which to proceed is to assume that he or she is sincere, honest, truthful and willing and anxious to pay the charges, once convinced they are correct. To put it differently and perhaps more clearly, people are honest and want to discharge their obligations. The exceptions to that rule are comparatively few, and I am convinced that the individuals who are inclined to chisel will in most cases react favorably if you make them feel that you consider them honest, upright and fair."

⇒ PRINCIPLE 10 ⇐

Appeal to the nobler motives.

↣ 20 ↢

"THE MOVIES DO IT. TV DOES IT. WHY DON'T YOU DO IT?"

Many years ago, the Philadelphia Evening Bulletin was being maligned by a dangerous whispering campaign. A malicious rumor was being circulated. Advertisers were being told that the newspaper was no longer attractive to readers because it carried too much advertising and too little news. Immediate action was necessary. The gossip had to be squelched.

But how?

This is the way it was done.

The Bulletin clipped from its regular edition all reading matter of all kinds on one average day, classified it, and published it as a book. The book was called One Day. It contained 307 pages—as many as a hard-covered book; yet the Bulletin had printed all this news and feature material in one day and sold it, not for several dollars, but for a few cents.

The printing of that book dramatized the fact that the Bulletin carried an enormous amount of interesting reading matter. It conveyed the facts more vividly, more interestingly, more impressively, than pages of figures and mere talk could have done.

This is the day of dramatization. Merely stating a truth isn't enough. The truth has to be made vivid, interesting, and dramatic. You have to use showmanship. The movies do it. Television does it. And you will have to do it if you want attention.

Experts in window display know the power of dramatization. For example, the manufacturers of a new rat poison gave dealers a window display that included two live rats. The week the rats were shown, sales zoomed to five times their normal rate.

Television commercials abound with examples of the use of dramatic techniques in selling products. Sit down one evening in front of your television set and analyze what the advertisers do in each of their presentations. You will note how an antacid medicine changes the color of the acid in a test tube while its competitor doesn't, how one brand of soap or detergent gets a greasy shirt clean when the other brand leaves it gray. You'll see a car maneuver around a series of turns and curves—far better than just being told about it. Happy faces will show contentment with a variety of products. All of these dramatize for the viewer the advantages offered by whatever is being sold—and they do get people to buy them.

You can dramatize your ideas in business or in any other aspect of your life. It's easy. Jim Yeamans, who sells for the NCR company (National Cash Register) in Richmond, Virginia, told how he made a sale by dramatic demonstration.

"Last week I called on a neighborhood grocer and saw that the cash registers he was using at his checkout counters were very old-fashioned. I approached the owner and told him, 'You are literally throwing away pennies every time a customer goes through your line.' With that I threw a handful of pennies on the floor. He quickly became more attentive. The mere words should have been of interest to him, but the sound of pennies hitting the floor really stopped him. I was able to get an order from him to replace all of his old machines."

It works in home life as well. When the old-time lover proposed to his sweetheart, did he just use words of love? No! He went down on his knees. That really showed he meant what he said. We don't propose on our knees any more, but many suitors still set up a romantic atmosphere before they pop the question.

Dramatizing what you want works with children as well. Joe B. Fant, Jr., of Birmingham, Alabama, was having difficulty getting his five-year-old boy and three-year-old daughter to pick up their toys, so he invented a 'train'. Joey was the engineer (Captain Casey Jones) on his tricycle. Janet's wagon was attached, and in the evening she loaded all the "coal" on the caboose (her wagon) and then jumped in while her brother drove her around the room. In this way the room was cleaned up—without lectures, arguments or threats.

Mary Catherine Wolf of Mishawaka, Indiana, was having some problems at work and decided that she had to discuss them with the boss. On Monday morning she requested an appointment with him but was told he was very busy and she should arrange with his secretary for an appointment later in the week. The secretary indicated that his schedule was very tight, but she would try to fit her in.

Ms. Wolf described what happened:

"I did not get a reply from her all week long. Whenever I questioned her, she would give me a reason why the boss could not see me. Friday morning came and I had heard nothing definite. I really wanted to see him and discuss my problems before the weekend, so I asked myself how I could get him to see me.

"What I finally did was this. I wrote him a formal letter. I indicated in the letter that I fully understood how extremely busy he was all week, but it was important that I speak with him. I enclosed a form letter and a self-addressed envelope and asked him to please fill it out or ask his secretary to do it and return it to me. The form letter read as follows:

Ms. Wolf, I will be able to see you on __________ at __________ A.M/P.M. I will give you __________ minutes of my time.

"I put this letter in his in-basket at 11 A.M. At 2 P.M. I checked my mailbox. There was my self-addressed envelope. He had answered my form letter himself and indicated he could see me that afternoon and could give me ten minutes of his time. I met with him, and we talked for over an hour and resolved my problems.

"If I had not dramatized to him the fact that I really wanted to see him, I would probably be still waiting for an appointment."

James B. Boynton had to present a lengthy market report. His firm had just finished an exhaustive study for a leading brand of cold cream. Data were needed immediately about the competition in this market; the prospective customer was one of the biggest—and most formidable—men in the advertising business.

And his first approach failed almost before he began.

"The first time I went in," Mr. Boynton explains, "I found myself sidetracked into a futile discussion of the methods used in the investigation. He argued and I argued. He told me I was wrong, and I tried to prove that I was right.

"I finally won my point, to my own satisfaction—but my time was up, the interview was over, and I still hadn't produced results.

"The second time, I didn't bother with tabulations of figures and data. I went to see this man. I dramatized my facts.

"As I entered his office, he was busy on the phone. While he finished his conversation, I opened a suitcase and dumped thirty-two jars of cold cream on top of his desk—all products he knew—all competitors of his cream.

"On each jar, I had a tag itemizing the results of the trade investigation. And each tag told its story briefly, dramatically.

"What happened?

"There was no longer an argument. Here was something new, something different. He picked up first one and then another of the jars of cold cream and read the information on the tag. A friendly conversation developed. He asked additional questions. He was intensely interested. He had originally given me only ten minutes to present my facts, but ten minutes passed, twenty minutes, forty minutes, and at the end of an hour we were still talking.

"I was presenting the same facts this time that I had presented previously. But this time I was using dramatization, showmanship—and what a difference it made."

⇒ PRINCIPLE 11 ⇐

Dramatize your ideas.

↣ 21 ↢

"WHEN NOTHING ELSE WORKS, TRY THIS."

Charles Schwab had a mill manager whose people weren't producing their quota of work.

"How is it," Schwab asked him, "that a manager as capable as you can't make this mill turn out what it should?"

"I don't know," the manager replied. "I've coaxed the men, I've pushed them, I've sworn and cussed, I've threatened them with damnation and being fired. But nothing works. They just won't produce."

This conversation took place at the end of the day, just before the night shift came on. Schwab asked the manager for a piece of chalk, then, turning to the nearest man, asked, "How many heats did your shift make today?"

"Six."

Without another word, Schwab chalked a big figure six on the floor, and walked away.

When the night shift came in, they saw the "6" and asked what it meant.

"The big boss was in here today," the day people said. "He asked us how many heats we made, and we told him six. He chalked it down on the floor."

The next morning Schwab walked through the mill again. The night shift had rubbed out "6" and replaced it with a big "7."

When the day shift reported for work the next morning, they saw a big "7" chalked on the floor. So the night shift thought they were better than the day shift did they? Well, they would show the night shift a thing or two. The crew pitched in with enthusiasm, and when they quit that night, they left behind them an enormous, swaggering "10". Things were stepping up.

Shortly this mill, which had been lagging way behind in production, was turning out more work than any other mill in the plant.

The principle?

Let Charles Schwab say it in his own words: "The way to get things done," said Schwab, "is to stimulate competition. I do not mean in a sordid, money-getting way, but in the desire to excel."

The desire to excel! The challenge! Throwing down the gauntlet! An infallible way of appealing to people of spirit.

Without a challenge, Theodore Roosevelt would never have been President of the United States. The Rough Rider, just back from Cuba, was picked for governor of New York State. The opposition discovered he was no longer a legal resident of the state, and Roosevelt, frightened, wished to withdraw. Then Thomas Collier Platt, then U.S. Senator from New York, threw down the challenge. Turning suddenly on Theodore Roosevelt, he cried in a ringing voice, "Is the hero of San Juan Hill a coward?"

Roosevelt stayed in the fight—and the rest is history. A challenge not only changed his life; it had a real effect upon the future of his nation.

"All men have fears, but the brave put down their fears and go forward, sometimes to death, but always to victory" was the motto of the King's Guard in ancient Greece. What greater challenge can be offered than the opportunity to overcome those fears?

When Al Smith was governor of New York, he was up against it. Sing Sing, at the time the most notorious penitentiary west of Devil's Island, was without a warden. Scandals had been sweeping through the pristine walls, scandals and ugly rumors. Smith needed a strong man to rule Sing Sing—an iron man. But who?

He sent for Lewis E. Lawes of New Hampton.

"How about going up to take charge of Sing Sing?" he said jovially when Lawes stood before him. "They need a man up there with experience."

Lawes was flabbergasted. He knew the dangers of Sing Sing. It was a political appointment, subject to the vagaries of political whims. Wardens had come and gone—one had lasted only three weeks. He had a career to consider. Was it worth the risk?

Then Smith, who saw his hesitation, leaned back in his chair and smiled. "Young fellow," he said, "I don't blame you for being scared. It's a tough spot. It'll take a big person to go up there and stay."

So Smith was throwing down a challenge, was he? Lawes liked the idea of attempting a job that called for someone "big".

So he went. And he stayed. He stayed, to become the most famous warden of his time. His book 20,000 Years in Sing Sing sold into the hundreds of thousands of copies. His broadcasts on the air and his stories of prison life have inspired dozens of movies. His "humanizing" of criminals wrought miracles in the way of prison reform.

"I have never found," said Harvey S. Firestone, founder of the great Firestone Tire and Rubber Company, "that pay and pay alone would either bring together or hold good people. I think it was the game itself."

Frederic Herzberg, one of the great behavioral scientists, concurred. He studied in depth the work attitudes of thousands of people ranging from factory workers to senior executives. What do you think he found to be the most motivating factor—the one facet of the jobs that was most stimulating? Money? Good working conditions? Fringe benefits? No, not any of those. The one major factor that motivated people was the work itself. If the work was exciting and interesting, the worker looked forward to doing it and was motivated to do a good job.

That is what every successful person loves: the game. The chance for self-expression. The chance to prove his or her worth, to excel, to win. That is what makes footraces and hog-calling and pie-eating contests. The desire to excel. The desire for a feeling of importancc.

⇒ PRINCIPLE 12 ⇐

Throw down a challenge.

In a Nutshell

HOW TO WIN PEOPLE TO YOUR WAY OF THINKING

⇒ PRINCIPLE 1 ⇐

The only way to get the best of an argument is to avoid it.

⇒ PRINCIPLE 2 ⇐

Show respect for the other person's opinions. Never say, "You're wrong."

⇒ PRINCIPLE 3 ⇐

If you are wrong, admit it quickly and emphatically.

⇒ PRINCIPLE 4 ⇐

Begin in a friendly way.

⇒ PRINCIPLE 5 ⇐

Get the other person saying "Yes, yes" immediately.

⇒ PRINCIPLE 6 ⇐

Let the other person do a great deal of the talking.

⇒ PRINCIPLE 7 ⇐

Let the other person feel that the idea is his or hers.

⇒ PRINCIPLE 8 ⇐

Try honestly to see things from the other person's point of view.

⇒ PRINCIPLE 9 ⇐

Be sympathetic with the other person's ideas and desires.

⇒ PRINCIPLE 10 ⇐

Appeal to the nobler motives.

⇒ PRINCIPLE 11 ⇐

Dramatize your ideas.

⇒ PRINCIPLE 12 ⇐

Throw down a challenge.

PART FOUR

Be A Leader: How To Change People Without Giving Offence Or Arousing Resentment

↣ 22 ↢

"IF YOU MUST FIND FAULT, THIS IS THE WAY TO BEGIN."

A friend of mine was a guest at the White House for a weekend during the administration of Calvin Coolidge. Drifting into the President's private office, he heard Coolidge say to one of his secretaries, "That's a pretty dress you are wearing this morning, and you are a very attractive young woman."

That was probably the most effusive praise Silent Cal had ever bestowed upon a secretary in his life. It was so unusual, so unexpected, that the secretary blushed in confusion. Then Coolidge said, "Now, don't get stuck up. I just said that to make you feel good. From now on, I wish you would be a little bit more careful with your punctuation."

His method was probably a bit obvious, but the psychology was superb. It is always easier to listen to unpleasant things after we have heard some praise of our good points.

A barber lathers a man before he shaves him; and that is precisely what McKinley did back in 1896, when he was running for President. One of the prominent Republicans of that day had written a campaign speech that he felt was just a trifle better than Cicero and Patrick Henry and Daniel Webster all rolled into one. With great glee, this chap read his immortal speech aloud to McKinley. The speech had its fine points, but it just wouldn't do. It would have raised a tornado of criticism. McKinley didn't want to hurt the man's feelings. He must not kill the man's splendid enthusiasm, and yet he had to say 'no'. Note how adroitly he did it.

"My friend, that is a splendid speech, a magnificent speech," McKinley said. "No one could have prepared a better one. There are many occasions on which it would be precisely the right thing to say, but is it quite suitable to this particular occasion? Sound and sober as it is from your standpoint, I must consider its effect from the party's standpoint. Now you go home and write a speech along the lines I indicate, and send me a copy of it."

He did just that. McKinley blue-penciled and helped him rewrite his second speech, and he became one of the effective speakers of the campaign.

Here is the second most famous letter that Abraham Lincoln ever wrote. (His most famous one was written to Mrs. Bixby, expressing his sorrow for the death of the five sons she had lost in battle.) Lincoln probably dashed this letter off in five minutes; yet it sold at public auction in 1926 for twelve thousand dollars, and that, by the way, was more money than Lincoln was able to save during half a century of hard work. The letter was written to General Joseph Hooker on April 26, 1863, during the darkest period of the Civil War. For eighteen months, Lincoln's generals had been leading the Union Army from one tragic defeat to another. Nothing but futile, stupid human butchery. The nation was appalled. Thousands of soldiers had deserted from the army, and then the Republican members of the Senate had revolted and wanted to force Lincoln out of the White House. "We are now on the brink of destruction," Lincoln said. It appears to me that even the Almighty is against us. I can hardly see a ray of hope." Such was the black sorrow and chaos out of which this letter came.

I am printing the letter here because it shows how Lincoln tried to change an obstreperous general when the very fate of the nation could have depended upon the general's action.

This is perhaps the sharpest letter Abe Lincoln wrote after he became President; yet you will note that he praised General Hooker before he spoke of his grave faults.

Yes, they were grave faults, but Lincoln didn't call them that. Lincoln was more conservative, more diplomatic. Lincoln wrote, "There are some things in regard to which I am not quite satisfied with you." Talk about tact! And diplomacy!

Here is the letter addressed to General Hooker:

I have placed you at the head of the Army of the Potomac.

Of course, I have done this upon what appears to me to be sufficient reasons, and yet I think it best for you to know that there are some things in regard to which I am not quite satisfied with you.

I believe you to be a brave and skillful soldier, which, of course, I like. I also believe you do not mix politics with your profession, in which you are right. You have confidence in yourself, which is a valuable if not an indispensable quality.

You are ambitious, which, within reasonable bounds, does good rather than harm. But I think that during General Burnside's command of the army you have taken counsel of your ambition and thwarted him as much as you could, in which you did a great wrong to the country and to a most meritorious and honorable brother officer.

I have heard, in such a way as to believe it, of you recently saying that both the army and the Government needed a dictator. Of course, it was not for this, but in spite of it, that I have given you command. Only those generals who gain success can be set up as dictators. What I now ask of you is military success and I will risk the dictatorship.

The Government will support you to the utmost of its ability, which is neither more nor less than it has done and will do for all commanders. I fear that the spirit which you have aided to infuse into the army, of criticizing their commander and withholding confidence from him, will now turn upon you. I shall assist you, as far as I can, to put it down.

Neither you nor Napoleon, if he were alive again, could get any good out of an army while such spirit prevails in it, and now beware of rashness. Beware of rashness, but with energy and sleepless vigilance go forward and give us victories.

You are not a Coolidge, a McKinley or a Lincoln. You want to know whether this philosophy will operate for you in everyday business contacts. Will it? Let's see. Let's take the case of W. P. Gaw of the Wark Company, Philadelphia.

The Wark Company had contracted to build and complete a large office building in Philadelphia by a certain specified date. Everything was going along well; the building was almost finished, when suddenly the subcontractor making the ornamental bronze work to go on the exterior of this building declared that he couldn't make delivery on schedule. What! An entire building held up! Heavy penalties! Distressing losses! All because of one man!

Long-distance telephone calls. Arguments! Heated conversations! All in vain. Then Mr. Gaw was sent to New York to beard the bronze lion in his den.

"Do you know you are the only person in Brooklyn with your name?" Mr. Gaw asked the president of the subcontracting firm shortly after they were introduced. The president was surprised. "No, I didn't know that."

"Well," said Mr. Gaw, "when I got off the train this morning, I looked in the telephone book to get your address, and you're the only person in the Brooklyn phone book with your name."

"I never knew that," the subcontractor said. He checked the phone book with interest. "Well, it's an unusual name," he said proudly. "My family came from Holland and settled in New York almost two hundred years ago." He continued to talk about his family and his ancestors for several minutes. When he finished that, Mr. Gaw complimented him on how large a plant he had and compared it favorably with a number of similar plants he had visited. "It is one of the cleanest and neatest bronze factories I ever saw," said Gaw.

"I've spent a lifetime building up this business," the subcontractor said, "and I am rather proud of it. Would you like to take a look around the factory?"

During this tour of inspection, Mr. Gaw complimented the other man on his system of fabrication and told him how and why it seemed superior to those of some of his competitors. Gaw commented on some unusual machines, and the subcontractor announced that he himself had invented those machines. He spent considerable time showing Gaw how they operated and the superior work they turned out. He insisted on taking his visitor to lunch. So far, mind you, not a word had been said about the real purpose of Gaw's visit.

After lunch, the subcontractor said, "Now, to get down to business. Naturally, I know why you're here. I didn't expect that our meeting would be so enjoyable. You can go back to Philadelphia with my promise that your material will be fabricated and shipped, even if other orders have to be delayed."

Mr. Gaw got everything that he wanted without even asking for it. The material arrived on time, and the building was completed on the day the completion contract specified.

Would this have happened had Mr. Gaw used the hammer-and-dynamite method generally employed on such occasions?

Dorothy Wrublewski, a branch manager of the Fort Monmouth, New Jersey, Federal Credit Union, reported to one of our classes how she was able to help one of her employees become more productive.

"We recently hired a young lady as a teller trainee. Her contact with our customers was very good. She was accurate and efficient in handling individual transactions. The problem developed at the end of the day when it was time to balance out.

"The head teller came to me and strongly suggested that I fire this woman. 'She is holding up everyone else because she is so slow in balancing out. I've shown her over and over, but she can't get it. She's got to go.'

"The next day I observed her working quickly and accurately when handling the normal everyday transactions, and she was very pleasant with our customers.

"It didn't take long to discover why she had trouble balancing out. After the office closed, I went over to talk with her. She was obviously nervous and upset. I praised her for being so friendly and outgoing with the customers and complimented her for the accuracy and speed used in that work. I then suggested we review the procedure we use in balancing the cash drawer. Once she realized I had confidence in her, she easily followed my suggestions and soon mastered this function. We have had no problems with her since then."

Beginning with praise is like the dentist who begins his work with Novocain. The patient still gets a drilling, but the Novocain is pain-killing. A leader will use...

⇒ PRINCIPLE 1 ⇐

Begin with praise and honest appreciation.

↣ 23 ↢

"HOW TO CRITICIZE—AND NOT BE HATED FOR IT."

Charles Schwab was passing through one of his steel mills one day at noon when he came across some of his employees smoking. Immediately above their heads was a sign that said "No Smoking." Did Schwab point to the sign and say, "Can't you read.? Oh no, not Schwab. He walked over to the men, handed each one a cigar, and said, "I'll appreciate it, boys, if you will smoke these on the outside." They knew that he knew that they had broken a rule—and they admired him because he said nothing about it and gave them a little present and made them feel important. Couldn't keep from loving a man like that, could you?

John Wanamaker used the same technique. Wanamaker used to make a tour of his great store in Philadelphia every day. Once he saw a customer waiting at a counter. No one was paying the slightest attention to her. The salespeople? Oh, they were in a huddle at the far end of the counter laughing and talking among themselves. Wanamaker didn't say a word. Quietly slipping behind the counter, he waited on the woman himself and then handed the purchase to the salespeople to be wrapped as he went on his way.

Public officials are often criticized for not being accessible to their constituents. They are busy people, and the fault sometimes lies in overprotective assistants who don't want to overburden their bosses with too many visitors. Carl Langford, who has been mayor of Orlando, Florida, the home of Disney World, for many years, frequently admonished his staff to allow people to see him, claimed he had an "open-door" policy; yet the citizens of his community were blocked by secretaries and administrators when they called.

Finally the mayor found the solution. He removed the door from his office! His aides got the message, and the mayor has had a truly open administration since the day his door was symbolically thrown away.

Simply changing one three-letter word can often spell the difference between failure and success in changing people without giving offense or arousing resentment.

Many people begin their criticism with sincere praise followed by the word "but" and ending with a critical statement. For example, in trying to change a child's careless attitude toward studies, we might say, "We're really proud of you, Johnnie, for raising your grades this term. But if you had worked harder on your algebra, the results would have been better."

In this case, Johnnie might feel encouraged until he heard the word "but". He might then question the sincerity of the original praise. To him, the praise seemed only to be a contrived lead-in to a critical inference of failure. Credibility would be strained, and we probably would not achieve our objectives of changing Johnnie's attitude toward his studies.

This could be easily overcome by changing the word "but" to "and". "We're really proud of you, Johnnie, for raising your grades this term, and by continuing the same conscientious efforts next term, your algebra grade can be up with all the others."

Now, Johnnie would accept the praise because there was no follow-up of an inference of failure. We have called his attention to the behavior we wished to change indirectly and the chances are he will try to live up to our expectations.

Calling attention to one's mistakes indirectly works wonders with sensitive people who may bitterly resent any direct criticism. Marge Jacob of Woonsocket, Rhode Island, told one of our classes how she convinced some sloppy construction workers to clean up after themselves when they were building additions to her house.

For the first few days of the work, when Mrs. Jacob returned from her job, she noticed that the yard was strewn with the cut ends of lumber. She didn't want to antagonize the builders, because they did excellent work. So after the workers had gone home, she and her children picked up and neatly piled all the lumber debris in a corner. The following morning she called the foreman to one side and said, "I'm really pleased with the way 109 the front lawn was left last night; it is nice and clean and does not offend the neighbors." From that day forward the workers picked up and piled the debris to one side, and the foreman came in each day seeking approval of the condition the lawn was left in after a day's work.

One of the major areas of controversy between members of the army reserves and their regular army trainers is haircuts. The reservists consider themselves civilians (which they are most of the time) and resent having to cut their hair short.

Master Sergeant Harley Kaiser of the 542nd USAR School addressed himself to this problem when he was working with a group of reserve noncommissioned officers. As an old-time regular-army master sergeant, he might have been expected to yell at his troops and threaten them. Instead he chose to make his point indirectly.

"Gentlemen," he started, "you are leaders. You will be most effective when you lead by example. You must be the example for your men to follow. You know what the army regulations say about haircuts. I am going to get my hair cut today, although it is still much shorter than some of yours. You look at yourself in the mirror, and if you feel you need a haircut to be a good example, we'll arrange time for you to visit the barbershop."

The result was predictable. Several of the candidates did look in the mirror and went to the barbershop that afternoon and received "regulation" haircuts. Sergeant Kaiser commented the next morning that he already could see the development of leadership qualities in some of the members of the squad.

On March 8, 1887, the eloquent Henry Ward Beecher died. The following Sunday, Lyman Abbott was invited to speak in the pulpit left silent by Beecher's passing. Eager to do his best, he wrote, rewrote and polished his sermon with the meticulous care of a Flaubert. Then he read it to his wife. It was poor - as most written speeches are. She might have said, if she had had less judgment, "Lyman, that is terrible. That'll never do. You'll put people to sleep. It reads like an encyclopedia. You ought to know better than that after all the years you have been preaching. For heaven's sake, why don't you talk like a human being? Why don't you act natural? You'll disgrace yourself if you ever read that stuff."

That's what she might have said. And, if she had, you know what would have happened. And she knew too. So, she merely remarked that it would make an excellent article for the North American Review. In other words, she praised it and at the same time subtly suggested that it wouldn't be done as a speech. Lyman Abbott saw the point, tore up his carefully prepared manuscript and preached without even using notes.

An effective way to correct others' mistakes is...

PRINCIPLE 2

Call attention to people's mistakes indirectly.

↣ 24 ↢

"TALK ABOUT YOUR OWN MISTAKES FIRST."

My niece, Josephine Carnegie, had come to New York to be my secretary. She was nineteen, had graduated from high school three years previously, and her business experience was a trifle more than zero. She became one of the most proficient secretaries west of Suez, but in the beginning, she was—well, susceptible to improvement. One day when I started to criticize her, I said to myself: "Just a minute, Dale Carnegie; just a minute. You are twice as old as Josephine. You have had ten thousand times as much business experience. How can you possibly expect her to have your viewpoint, your judgment, your initiative—mediocre though they may be? And just a minute, Dale, what were you doing at nineteen? Remember the asinine mistakes and blunders you made? Remember the time you did this...and that...?"

After thinking the matter over, honestly and impartially, I concluded that Josephine's batting average at nineteen was better than mine had been—and that, I'm sorry to confess, isn't paying Josephine much of a compliment.

So after that, when I wanted to call Josephine's attention to a mistake, I used to begin by saying, "You have made a mistake, Josephine, but the Lord knows, it's no worse than many I have made. You were not born with judgment. That comes only with experience, and you are better than I was at your age. I have been guilty of so many stupid, silly things myself, I have very little inclination to criticize you or anyone. But don't you think it would have been wiser if you had done so and so?"

It isn't nearly so difficult to listen to a recital of your faults if the person criticizing begins by humbly admitting that he, too, is far from impeccable.

E. G. Dillistone, an engineer in Brandon, Manitoba, Canada, was having problems with his new secretary. Letters he dictated were coming to his desk for signature with two or three spelling mistakes per page. Mr. Dillistone reported how he handled this:

"Like many engineers, I have not been noted for my excellent English or spelling. For years I have kept a little black thumb index book for words I had trouble spelling. When it became apparent that merely pointing out the errors was not going to cause my secretary to do more proofreading and dictionary work, I resolved to take another approach. When the next letter came to my attention that had errors in it, I sat down with the typist and said:

"'Somehow this word doesn't look right. It's one of the words I always have had trouble with. That's the reason I started this spelling book of mine. [I opened the book to the appropriate page.] Yes, here it is. I'm very conscious of my spelling now because people judge us by our letters and misspellings make us look less professional.

"I don't know whether she copied my system or not, but since that conversation, her frequency of spelling errors has been significantly reduced."

The polished Prince Bernhard von Bülow learned the sharp necessity of doing this back in 1909. Von Bülow was then the Imperial Chancellor of Germany, and on the throne sat Wilhelm II—Wilhelm, the haughty; Wilhelm the arrogant; Wilhelm, the last of the German Kaisers, building an army and navy that he boasted could whip their weight in wildcats.

Then an astonishing thing happened. The Kaiser said things, incredible things, things that rocked the continent and started a series of explosions heard around the world. To make matters infinitely worse, the Kaiser made silly, egotistical, absurd announcements in public, he made them while he was a guest in England, and he gave his royal permission to have them printed in the *Daily Telegraph*. For example, he declared that he was the only German who felt friendly toward the English; that he was constructing a navy against the menace of Japan; that he, and he alone, had saved England from being humbled in the dust by Russia and France; that it had been his campaign plan that enabled England's Lord Roberts to defeat the Boers in South Africa; and so on and on.

No other such amazing words had ever fallen from the lips of a European king in peacetime within a hundred years. The entire continent buzzed with the fury of a hornet's nest. England was incensed. German statesmen were aghast. And in the midst of all this consternation, the Kaiser became panicky and suggested to Prince von Bülow, the Imperial Chancellor, that he take the blame. Yes, he wanted von Bülow to announce that it was all his responsibility, that he had advised his monarch to say these incredible things.

"But Your Majesty," von Bülow protested, "it seems to me utterly impossible that anybody either in Germany or England could suppose me capable of having advised Your Majesty to say any such thing."

The moment those words were out of von Bülow's mouth, he realized he had made a grave mistake. The Kaiser blew up.

"You consider me a donkey," he shouted, "capable of blunders you yourself could never have committed!"

Von Bülow knew that he ought to have praised before he condemned; but since that was too late, he did the next best thing. He praised after he had criticized. And it worked a miracle.

"I'm far from suggesting that," he answered respectfully. "Your Majesty surpasses me in many respects; not only of course, in naval and military knowledge but above all, in natural science. I have often listened in admiration when Your Majesty explained the barometer, or wireless telegraphy, or the Roentgen rays. I am shamefully ignorant of all branches of natural science, have no notion of chemistry or physics, and am quite incapable of explaining the simplest of natural phenomena. But," von Bülow continued, "in compensation, I possess some historical knowledge and perhaps certain qualities useful in politics, especially in diplomacy."

The Kaiser beamed. Von Bülow had praised him. Von Bülow had exalted him and humbled himself. The Kaiser could forgive anything after that. "Haven't I always told you," he exclaimed with enthusiasm, "that we complete one another famously? We should stick together, and we will!"

He shook hands with von Bülow, not once, but several times. And later in the day he waxed so enthusiastically that he exclaimed with doubled fists, "If anyone says anything to me against Prince von Bülow, I shall punch him in the nose."

Von Bülow saved himself in time—but, canny diplomat that he was, he nevertheless had made one error: he should have begun by talking about his own shortcomings and Wilhelm's superiority - not by intimating that the Kaiser was a half-wit in need of a guardian.

If a few sentences humbling oneself and praising the other party can turn a haughty, insulted Kaiser into a staunch friend, imagine what humility and praise can do for you and me in our daily contacts. Rightfully used, they will work veritable miracles in human relations.

Admitting one's own mistakes—even when one hasn't corrected them—can help convince somebody to change his behavior. This was illustrated more recently by Clarence Zerhusen of Timonium, Maryland, when he discovered his fifteen-year-old son was experimenting with cigarettes.

"Naturally, I didn't want David to smoke," Mr. Zerhusen told us, "but his mother and I smoked cigarettes; we were giving him a bad example all the time. I explained to Dave how I started smoking at about his age and how the nicotine had gotten the best of me and now it was nearly impossible for me to stop. I reminded him how irritating my cough was and how he had been after me to give up cigarettes not many years before.

"I didn't exhort him to stop or make threats or warn him about their dangers. All I did was point out how I was hooked on cigarettes and what it had meant to me.

"He thought about it for a while and decided he wouldn't smoke until he had graduated from high school. As the years went by David never did start smoking and has no intention of ever doing so.

"As a result of that conversation I made the decision to stop smoking cigarettes myself, and with the support of my family, I have succeeded."

A good leader follows this principle:

⇒ PRINCIPLE 3 ⇐

Talk about your own mistakes before criticizing the other person.

↣ 25 ↢

"NO ONE LIKES TO TAKE ORDERS."

I once had the pleasure of dining with Miss Ida Tarbell, the dean of American biographers. When I told her I was writing this book, we began discussing this all-important subject of getting along with people, and she told me that while she was writing her biography of Owen D. Young, she interviewed a man who had sat for three years in the same office with Mr. Young. This man declared that during all that time he had never heard Owen D. Young give a direct order to anyone. He always gave suggestions, not orders. Owen D. Young never said, for example, "Do this or do that," or "Don't do this or don't do that." He would say, "You might consider this," or "Do you think that would work?" Frequently he would say, after he had dictated a letter, "What do you think of this?" In looking over a letter of one of his assistants, he would say, "Maybe if we were to phrase it this way it would be better." He always gave people the opportunity to do things themselves; he never told his assistants to do things; he let them do them, let them learn from their mistakes.

A technique like that makes it easy for a person to correct errors. A technique like that saves a person's pride and gives him or her a feeling of importance. It encourages cooperation instead of rebellion.

Resentment caused by a brash order may last a long time—even if the order was given to correct an obviously bad situation. Dan Santarelli, a teacher at a vocational school in Wyoming, Pennsylvania, told one of our classes how one of his students had blocked the entranceway to one of the school's shops by illegally parking his car in it. One of the other instructors stormed into the classroom and asked in an arrogant tone, "Whose car is blocking the driveway?" When the student who owned the car responded, the instructor screamed: "Move that car and move it right now, or I'll wrap a chain around it and drag it out of there."

Now that student was wrong. The car should not have been parked there. But from that day on, not only did that student resent the instructor's action, but all the students in the class did everything they could to give the instructor a hard time and make his job unpleasant.

How could he have handled it differently? If he had asked in a friendly way, "Whose car is in the driveway?" and then suggested that if it were moved, other cars could get in and out, the student would have gladly moved it and neither he nor his classmates would have been upset and resentful.

Asking questions not only makes an order more palatable; it often stimulates the creativity of the persons whom you ask. People are more likely to accept an order if they have had a part in the decision that caused the order to be issued.

When Ian Macdonald of Johannesburg, South Africa, the general manager of a small manufacturing plant specializing in precision machine parts, had the opportunity to accept a very large order, he was convinced that he would not meet the promised delivery date. The work already scheduled in the shop and the short completion time needed for this order made it seem impossible for him to accept the order.

Instead of pushing his people to accelerate their work and rush the order through, he called everybody together, explained the situation to them, and told them how much it would mean to the company and to them if they could make it possible to produce the order on time. Then he started asking questions:

"Is there anything we can do to handle this order?"

"Can anyone think of different ways to process it through the shop that will make it possible to take the order?"

"Is there any way to adjust our hours or personnel assignments that would help?"

The employees came up with many ideas and insisted that he take the order. They approached it with a "We can do it" attitude, and the order was accepted, produced and delivered on time.

An effective leader will use...

⇒ PRINCIPLE 4 ⇐

Ask questions instead of giving direct orders.

↣ 26 ↢

"LET THE OTHER PERSON SAVE FACE."

Years ago the General Electric Company was faced with the delicate task of removing Charles Steinmetz from the head of a department. Steinmetz, a genius of the first magnitude when it came to electricity, was a failure as the head of the calculating department. Yet the company didn't dare offend the man. He was indispensable—and highly sensitive. So they gave him a new title. They made him Consulting Engineer of the General Electric Company—a new title for work he was already doing—and let someone else head up the department.

Steinmetz was happy.

So were the officers of G.E. They had gently maneuvered their most temperamental star, and they had done it without a storm—by letting him save face.

Letting one save face! How important, how vitally important that is! And how few of us ever stop to think of it! We ride roughshod over the feelings of others, getting our own way, finding fault, issuing threats, criticizing a child or an employee in front of others, without even considering the hurt to the other person's pride. Whereas a few minutes' thought, a considerate word or two, a genuine understanding of the other person's attitude, would go so far toward alleviating the sting!

Let's remember that the next time we are faced with the distasteful necessity of discharging or reprimanding an employee.

"Firing employees is not much fun. Getting fired is even less fun." (I'm quoting now from a letter written to me by Marshall A. Granger, a certified public accountant.) "Our business is mostly seasonal. Therefore we have to let a lot of people go after the income tax rush is over.

It's a byword in our profession that no one enjoys wielding the ax. Consequently, the custom has developed of getting it over as soon as possible, and usually in the following way: 'Sit down, Mr. Smith. The season's over, and we don't seem to see any more assignments for you. Of course, you understood you were only employed for the busy season anyhow, etc., etc.'

"The effect on these people is one of disappointment and a feeling of being 'let down.' Most of them are in the accounting field for life, and they retain no particular love for the firm that drops them so casually.

"I recently decided to let our seasonal personnel go with a little more tact and consideration. So I call each one in only after carefully thinking over his or her work during the winter. And I've said something like this: 'Mr. Smith, you've done a fine job (if he has). That time we sent you to Newark, you had a tough assignment. You were on the spot, but you came through with flying colors, and we want you to know the firm is proud of you. You've got the stuff—you're going a long way, wherever you're working. This firm believes in you, and is rooting for you, and we don't want you to forget it.'

"Effect? The people go away feeling a lot better about being fired. They don't feel 'let down.' They know if we had work for them, we'd keep them on. And when we need them again, they come to us with a keen personal affection."

At one session of our course, two class members discussed the negative effects of faultfinding versus the positive effects of letting the other person save face.

Fred Clark of Harrisburg, Pennsylvania, told of an incident that occurred in his company: "At one of our production meetings, a vice president was asking very pointed questions of one of our production supervisors regarding a production process. His tone of voice was aggressive and aimed at pointing out faulty performance on the part of the supervisor. Not wanting to be embarrassed in front of his peers, the supervisor was evasive in his responses. This caused the vice president to lose his temper, berate the supervisor and accuse him of lying.

"Any working relationship that might have existed prior to this encounter was destroyed in a few brief moments. This supervisor, who was basically a good worker, was useless to our company from that time on. A few months later he left our firm and went to work for a competitor, where I understand he is doing a fine job."

Another class member, Anna Mazzone, related how a similar incident had occurred at her job - but what a difference in approach and results! Ms. Mazzone, a marketing specialist for a food packer, was given her first major assignment—the test-marketing of a new product. She told the class: "When the results of the test came in, I was devastated. I had made a serious error in my planning, and the entire test had to be done all over again. To make this worse, I had no time to discuss it with my boss before the meeting in which I was to make my report on the project.

"When I was called on to give the report, I was shaking with fright. I had all I could do to keep from breaking down, but I resolved I would not cry and have all those men make remarks about women not being able to handle a management job because they are too emotional. I made my report briefly and stated that due to an error I would repeat the study before the next meeting. I sat down, expecting my boss to blow up.

"Instead, he thanked me for my work and remarked that it was not unusual for a person to make an error on a new project and that he had confidence that the repeat survey would be accurate and meaningful to the company. He assured me, in front of all my colleagues, that he had faith in me and I knew I had done my best, and that my lack of experience, not my lack of ability, was the reason for the failure.

I left that meeting with my head in the air and with the determination that I would never let that boss of mine down again."

Even if we are right and the other person is definitely wrong, we only destroy ego by causing someone to lose face. The legendary French aviation pioneer and author Antoine de Saint-Exupéry wrote: "I have no right to say or do anything that diminishes a man in his own eyes. What matters is not what I think of him, but what he thinks of himself. Hurting a man in his dignity is a crime."

A real leader will always follow...

⇒ PRINCIPLE 5 ⇐

Let the other person save face.

↣ 27 ↢

"HOW TO SPUR PEOPLE ON TO SUCCESS."

Pete Barlow was an old friend of mine. He had a dog-and-pony act and spent his life traveling with circuses and vaudeville shows. I loved to watch Pete train new dogs for his act. I noticed that the moment a dog showed the slightest improvement, Pete patted and praised him and gave him meat and made a great to-do about it.

That's nothing new. Animal trainers have been using that same technique for centuries.

Why, I wonder, don't we use the same common sense when trying to change people that we use when trying to change dogs? Why don't we use meat instead of a whip? Why don't we use praise instead of condemnation? Let us praise even the slightest improvement. That inspires the other person to keep on improving.

In his book *I Ain't Much, Baby—But I'm All I Got*, the psychologist Jess Lair comments, "Praise is like sunlight to the warm human spirit; we cannot flower and grow without it. And yet, while most of us are only too ready to apply to others the cold wind of criticism, we are somehow reluctant to give our fellow people the warm sunshine of praise." *

* Jess Lair, I Ain't Much, Baby—But I'm All I Got (Greenwich, Conn.: Fawcett, 1976), p . 248.

I can look back at my own life and see where a few words of praise have sharply changed my entire future. Can't you say the same thing about your life? History is replete with striking illustrations of the sheer witchery of praise.

For example, many years ago a boy of ten was working in a factory in Naples. He longed to be a singer, but his first teacher discouraged him. "You can't sing," he said. "You haven't any voice at all. It sounds like the wind in the shutters."

But his mother, a poor peasant woman, put her arms about him and praised him and told him she knew he could sing, she could already see an improvement, and she went barefoot in order to save money to pay for his music lessons. That peasant mother's praise and encouragement changed that boy's life. His name was Enrico Caruso, and he became the greatest and most famous opera singer of his age.

In the early nineteenth century, a young man in London aspired to be a writer. But everything seemed to be against him. He had never been able to attend school for more than four years. His father had been flung in jail because he couldn't pay his debts, and this young man often knew the pangs of hunger. Finally, he got a job pasting labels on bottles of blacking in a rat-infested warehouse, and he slept at night in a dismal attic room with two other boys—guttersnipes from the slums of London. He had so little confidence in his ability to write that he sneaked out and mailed his first manuscript in the dead of night so nobody would laugh at him. Story after story was refused. Finally the great day came when one was accepted. True, he wasn't paid a shilling for it, but one editor had praised him. One editor had given him recognition. He was so thrilled that he wandered aimlessly around the streets with tears rolling down his cheeks.

The praise, the recognition, that he received through getting one story in print, changed his whole life, for if it hadn't been for that encouragement, he might have spent his entire life working in rat-infested factories. You may have heard of that boy. His name was Charles Dickens.

Another boy in London made his living as a clerk in a dry-goods store. He had to get up at five o'clock, sweep out the store, and slave for fourteen hours a day. It was sheer drudgery and he despised it. After two years, he could no longer stand it, so he got up one morning and, without waiting for breakfast, tramped fifteen miles to talk to his mother, who was working as a housekeeper.

He was frantic. He pleaded with her. He wept. He swore he would kill himself if he had to remain in the shop any longer. Then he wrote a long, pathetic letter to his old schoolmaster, declaring that he was heartbroken, that he no longer wanted to live. His old schoolmaster gave him a little praise and assured him that he really was very intelligent and fitted for finer things and offered him a job as a teacher.

That praise changed the future of that boy and made a lasting impression on the history of English literature. For that boy went on to write innumerable best-selling books and made over a million dollars with his pen. You've probably heard of him. His name: H. G. Wells.

Use of praise instead of criticism is the basic concept of B. F. Skinner's teachings. This great contemporary psychologist has shown by experiments with animals and with humans that when criticism is minimized and praise emphasized, the good things people do will be reinforced and the poorer things will atrophy for lack of attention.

John Ringelspaugh of Rocky Mount, North Carolina, used this in dealing with his children. It seemed that, as in so many families, mother and dad's chief form of communication with the children was yelling at them. And, as in so many cases, the children became a little worse rather than better after each such session - and so did the parents. There seemed to be no end in sight for this problem.

Mr. Ringelspaugh was determined to use some of the principles he was learning in our course to solve this situation. He reported, "We decided to try praise instead of harping on their faults. It wasn't easy when all we could see were the negative things they were doing; it was really tough to find things to praise. We managed to find something, and within the first day or two some of the really upsetting things they were doing quit happening. Then some of their other faults began to disappear. They began capitalizing on the praise we were giving them. They even began going out of their way to do things right. Neither of us could believe it. Of course, it didn't last forever, but the norm reached after things leveled off was so much better. It was no longer necessary to react the way we used to. The children were doing far more right than wrong." All of this was a result of praising the slightest improvement in the children rather than condemning everything they did wrong.

This works on the job too. Keith Roper of Woodland Hills, California, applied this principle to a situation in his company. Some material came to him in his print shop which was of exceptionally high quality. The printer who had done this job was a new employee who had been having difficulty adjusting to the job. His supervisor was upset about what he considered a negative attitude and was seriously thinking of terminating his services.

When Mr. Roper was informed of this situation, he personally went over to the print shop and had a talk with the young man. He told him how pleased he was with the work he had just received and pointed out it was the best work he had seen produced in that shop for some time. He pointed out exactly why it was superior and how important the young man's contribution was to the company.

Do you think this affected that young printer's attitude toward the company? Within days there was a complete turnabout. He told several of his co-workers about the conversation and how someone in the company really appreciated good work. And from that day on, he was a loyal and dedicated worker.

What Mr. Roper did was not just flatter the young printer and say, "You're good." He specifically pointed out how his work was superior. Because he had singled out a specific accomplishment, rather than just making general flattering remarks, his praise became much more meaningful to the person to whom it was given. Everybody likes to be praised, but when praise is specific, it comes across as sincere—not something the other person may be saying just to make one feel good.

Remember, we all crave appreciation and recognition, and will do almost anything to get it. But nobody wants insincerity. Nobody wants flattery.

Let me repeat: The principles taught in this book will work only when they come from the heart. I am not advocating a bag of tricks. I am talking about a new way of life.

Talk about changing people. If you and I will inspire the people with whom we come in contact to a realization of the hidden treasures they possess, we can do far more than change people. We can literally transform them.

Exaggeration? Then listen to these sage words from William James, one of the most distinguished psychologists and philosophers America has ever produced: "Compared with what we ought to be, we are only half awake. We are making use of only a small part of our physical and mental resources. Stating the thing broadly, the human individual thus lives far within his limits. He possesses powers of various sorts which he habitually fails to use."

Yes, you who are reading these lines possess powers of various sorts which you habitually fail to use; and one of these powers you are probably not using to the fullest extent is your magic ability to praise people and inspire them with a realization of their latent possibilities.

Abilities wither under criticism; they blossom under encouragement. To become a more effective leader of people, apply...

⇒ PRINCIPLE 6 ⇐

Praise the slightest improvement and praise every improvement. Be "hearty in your approbation and lavish in your praise."

↣ 28 ↢

"GIVE A DOG A GOOD NAME."

What do you do when a person who has been a good worker begins to turn in shoddy work? You can fire him or her, but that really doesn't solve anything. You can berate the worker, but this usually causes resentment. Henry Henke, a service manager for a large truck dealership in Lowell, Indiana, had a mechanic whose work had become less than satisfactory. Instead of bawling him out or threatening him, Mr. Henke called him into his office and had a heart-to-heart talk with him.

"Bill," he said, "you are a fine mechanic. You have been in this line of work for a good number of years. You have repaired many vehicles to the customers' satisfaction. In fact, we've had a number of compliments about the good work you have done. Yet, of late, the time you take to complete each job has been increasing and your work has not been up to your own old standards. Because you have been such an outstanding mechanic in the past, I felt sure you would want to know that I am not happy with this situation, and perhaps jointly we could find some way to correct the problem."

Bill responded that he hadn't realized he had been falling down in his duties and assured his boss that the work he was getting was not out of his range of expertise and he would try to improve in the future.

Did he do it? You can be sure he did. He once again became a fast and thorough mechanic. With that reputation Mr. Henke had given him to live up to, how could he do anything else but turn out work comparable to that which he had done in the past.

"The average person," said Samuel Vauclain, then president of the Baldwin Locomotive Works, "can be led readily if you have his or her respect and if you show that you respect that person for some kind of ability."

In short, if you want to improve a person in a certain aspect, act as though that particular trait were already one of his or her outstanding characteristics. Shakespeare said, "Assume a virtue, if you have it not."

And it might be good to assume and state openly that other people have the virtue you want them to develop. Give them a fine reputation to live up to, and they will make prodigious efforts rather than see you disillusioned.

Georgette Leblanc, in her book *Souvenirs, My Life with Maeterlinck*, describes the startling transformation of a humble Belgian Cinderella.

"A servant girl from a neighboring hotel brought my meals," she wrote. "She was called 'Marie the Dishwasher' because she had started her career as a scullery assistant. She was a kind of monster, cross-eyed, bandy-legged, poor in flesh and spirit.

"One day, while she was holding my plate of macaroni in her red hand, I said to her point-blank, 'Marie, you do not know what treasures are within you.'

"Accustomed to holding back her emotion, Marie waited a few moments, not daring to risk the slightest gesture for fear of a catastrophe. Then she put the dish on the table, sighed and said ingenuously, 'Madame, I would never have believed it.' She did not doubt, she did not ask a question. She simply went back to the kitchen and repeated what I had said, and such is the force of faith that no one made fun of her. From that day on, she was even given a certain consideration. But the most curious change of all occurred in the humble Marie herself. Believing she was the tabernacle of unseen marvels, she began taking care of her face and body so carefully that her starved youth seemed to bloom and modestly hide her plainness.

"Two months later, she announced her coming marriage with the nephew of the chef. 'I'm going to be a lady,' she said, and thanked me. A small phrase had changed her entire life."

Georgette Leblanc had given "Marie the Dishwasher" a reputation to live up to—and that reputation had transformed her.

Bill Parker, a sales representative for a food company in Daytona Beach, Florida, was very excited about the new line of products his company was introducing and was upset when the manager of a large independent food market turned down the opportunity to carry it in his store. Bill brooded all day over this rejection and decided to return to the store before he went home that evening and try again.

"Jack," he said, "since I left this morning I realized I hadn't given you the entire picture of our new line, and I would appreciate some of your time to tell you about the points I omitted. I have respected the fact that you are always willing to listen and are big enough to change your mind when the facts warrant a change."

Could Jack refuse to give him another hearing? Not with that reputation to live up to.

One morning Dr. Martin Fitzhugh, a dentist in Dublin, Ireland, was shocked when one of his patients pointed out to him that the metal cup holder which she was using to rinse her mouth was not very clean. True, the patient drank from the paper cup, not the holder, but it certainly was not professional to use tarnished equipment.

When the patient left, Dr. Fitzhugh retreated to his private office to write a note to Bridgit, the chairwoman, who came twice a week to clean his office. He wrote:

"My dear Bridgit,

"I see you so seldom, I thought I'd take the time to thank you for the fine job of cleaning you've been doing. By the way, I thought I'd mention that since two hours, twice a week, is a very limited amount of time, please feel free to work an extra half-hour from time to time if you feel you need to do those 'once-in-a-while' things like polishing the cup holders and the like. I, of course, will pay you for the extra time."

"The next day, when I walked into my office," Dr. Fitzhugh reported, "My desk had been polished to a mirror-like finish, as had my chair, which I nearly slid out of. When I went into the treatment room I found the shiniest, cleanest chrome-plated cup holder I had ever seen nestled in its receptacle. I had given my charwoman a fine reputation to live up to, and because of this small gesture she outperformed all her past efforts. How much additional time did she spend on this? That's right—none at all."

There is an old saying: "Give a dog a bad name and you may as well hang him." But give him a good name—and see what happens!

When Mrs. Ruth Hopkins, a fourth-grade teacher in Brooklyn, New York, looked at her class roster the first day of school, her excitement and joy of starting a new term was tinged with anxiety. In her class this year she would have Tommy T., the school's most notorious "bad boy". His third-grade teacher had constantly complained about Tommy to colleagues, the principal and anyone else who would listen. He was not just mischievous; he caused serious discipline problems in the class, picked fights with the boys, teased the girls, was fresh to the teacher, and seemed to get worse as he grew older. His only redeeming feature was his ability to learn rapidly and master the schoolwork easily.

Mrs. Hopkins decided to face the "Tommy problem" immediately. When she greeted her new students, she made little comments to each of them: "Rose, that's a pretty dress you are wearing," "Alicia, I hear you draw beautifully." When she came to Tommy, she looked him straight in the eyes and said, "Tommy, I understand you are a natural leader. I'm going to depend on you to help me make this class the best class in the fourth grade this year." She reinforced this over the first few days by complimenting Tommy on everything he did and commenting on how this showed what a good student he was. With that reputation to live up to, even a nine-year-old couldn't let her down—and he didn't.

If you want to excel in that difficult leadership role of changing the attitude or behavior of others, use...

⇒ PRINCIPLE 7 ⇐

Give the other person a fine reputation to live up to.

↣ 29 ↢

"MAKE THE FAULT SEEM EASY TO CORRECT."

A bachelor friend of mine, about forty years old, became engaged, and his fiancée persuaded him to take some belated dancing lessons. "The Lord knows I needed dancing lessons," he confessed as he told me the story, "for I danced just as I did when I first started twenty years ago. The first teacher I engaged probably told me the truth. She said I was all wrong; I would just have to forget everything and begin all over again. But that took the heart out of me. I had no incentive to go on. So I quit her.

"The next teacher may have been lying, but I liked it. She said nonchalantly that my dancing was a bit old-fashioned perhaps, but the fundamentals were all right, and she assured me I wouldn't have any trouble learning a few new steps. The first teacher had discouraged me by emphasizing my mistakes. This new teacher did the opposite. She kept praising the things I did right and minimizing my errors. 'You have a natural sense of rhythm,' she assured me. 'You really are a natural-born dancer.' Now my common sense tells me that I always have been and always will be a fourth-rate dancer; yet, deep in my heart, I still like to think that maybe she meant it. To be sure, I was paying her to say it; but why bring that up?

"At any rate, I know I am a better dancer than I would have been if she hadn't told me I had a natural sense of rhythm. That encouraged me. That gave me hope. That made me want to improve."

Tell your child, your spouse, or your employee that he or she is stupid or dumb at a certain thing, has no gift for it, and is doing it all wrong, and you have destroyed almost every incentive to try to improve. But use the opposite technique—be liberal with your encouragement, make the thing seem easy to do, let the other person know that you have faith in his ability to do it, that he has an undeveloped flair for it - and he will practice until the dawn comes in the window in order to excel.

Lowell Thomas, a superb artist in human relations, used this technique. He gave you confidence, inspired you with courage and faith. For example, I spent a weekend with Mr. and Mrs. Thomas; and on Saturday night, I was asked to sit in on a friendly bridge game before a roaring fire. Bridge? Oh, no! No! No! Not me. I knew nothing about it. The game had always been a black mystery to me. No! No! Impossible!

"Why, Dale, it is no trick at all," Lowell replied. "There is nothing to bridge except memory and judgment. You've written articles on memory. The bridge will be a cinch for you. It's right up your alley."

And presto, almost before I realized what I was doing, I found myself for the first time at a bridge table. All because I was told I had a natural flair for it and the game was made to seem easy.

Speaking of bridges reminds me of Ely Culbertson, whose books on bridge have been translated into a dozen languages and have sold more than a million copies. Yet he told me he never would have made a profession out of the game if a certain young woman hadn't assured him he had a flair for it.

When he came to America in 1922, he tried to get a job teaching in philosophy and sociology, but he couldn't. Then he tried selling coal, and he failed at that

Then he tried selling coffee, and he failed at that, too.

He had played some bridge, but it had never occurred to him in those days that someday he would teach it. He was not only a poor card player, but he was also very stubborn. He asked so many questions and held so many post-mortem examinations that no one wanted to play with him.

Then he met a pretty bridge teacher, Josephine Dillon, fell in love and married her. She noticed how carefully he analyzed his cards and persuaded him that he was a potential genius at the card table. It was that encouragement and that alone, Culbertson told me, that caused him to make a profession of bridge.

Clarence M. Jones, one of the instructors of our course in Cincinnati, Ohio, told how encouragement and making faults seem easy to correct completely changed the life of his son.

"In 1970 my son David, who was then fifteen years old, came to live with me in Cincinnati. He had led a rough life. In 1958 his head was cut open in a car accident, leaving a very bad scar on his forehead. In 1960 his mother and I were divorced and he moved to Dallas, Texas, with his mother. Until he was fifteen he had spent most of his school years in special classes for slow learners in the Dallas school system. Possibly because of the scar, school administrators had decided he was brain-injured and could not function at a normal level. He was two years behind his age group, so he was only in the seventh grade. Yet he did not know his multiplication tables, added on his fingers and could barely read.

"There was one positive point. He loved to work on radio and TV sets. He wanted to become a TV technician. I encouraged this and pointed out that he needed math to qualify for the training. I decided to help him become proficient in this subject. We obtained four sets of flash cards: multiplication, division, addition and subtraction. As we went through the cards, we put the correct answers in a discard stack. When David missed one, I gave him the correct answer and then put the card in the repeat stack until there were no cards left. I made a big deal out of each card he got right, particularly if he had missed it previously. Each night we would go through the repeat stack until there were no cards left.

Each night we timed the exercise with a stopwatch. I promised him that when he could get all the cards correct in eight minutes with no incorrect answers, we would quit doing it every night. This seemed an impossible goal to David. The first night it took 52 minutes, the second night, 48, then 45, 44, 41 then under 40 minutes. We celebrated each reduction. I'd call in my wife, and we would both hug him and we'd all dance a jig. At the end of the month he was doing all the cards perfectly in less than eight minutes. When he made a small improvement he would ask to do it again. He had made the fantastic discovery that learning was easy and fun.

"Naturally his grades in algebra took a jump. It is amazing how much easier algebra is when you can multiply. He astonished himself by bringing home a B in math. That had never happened before. Other changes came with almost unbelievable rapidity. His reading improved rapidly, and he began to use his natural talents in drawing. Later in the school year his science teacher assigned him to develop an exhibit. He chose to develop a highly complex series of models to demonstrate the effect of levers. It required skill not only in drawing and model-making but in applied mathematics. The exhibit took first prize in his school's science fair and was entered in the city competition and won third prize for the entire city of Cincinnati.

"That did it. Here was a kid who had flunked two grades, who had been told he was 'brain-damaged,' who had been called 'Frankenstein' by his classmates and told his brains must have leaked out of the cut on his head. Suddenly he discovered he could really learn and accomplish things. The result? From the last quarter of the eighth grade all the way through high school, he never failed to make the honor roll; in high school he was elected to the National Honor Society. Once he found learning was easy, his whole life changed."

If you want to help others to improve, remember...

⇒ PRINCIPLE 8 ⇐

Use encouragement. Make the fault seem easy to correct.

↣ 30 ↢

"MAKING PEOPLE GLAD TO DO WHAT YOU WANT."

Back in 1915, America was aghast. For more than a year, the nations of Europe had been slaughtering one another on a scale never before dreamed of in all the bloody annals of mankind. Could peace be brought about? No one knew. But Woodrow Wilson was determined to try. He would send a personal representative, a peace emissary, to counsel with the warlords of Europe.

William Jennings Bryan, secretary of state, Bryan, the peace advocate, longed to go. He saw a chance to perform a great service and make his name immortal. But Wilson appointed another man, his intimate friend and advisor Colonel Edward M. House; and it was House's thorny task to break the unwelcome news to Bryan without giving him offense.

"Bryan was distinctly disappointed when he heard I was to go to Europe as the peace emissary," Colonel House records in his diary. "He said he had planned to do this himself...

"I replied that the President thought it would be unwise for anyone to do this officially, and that his going would attract a great deal of attention and people would wonder why he was there..."

You see the intimation? House practically told Bryan that he was too important for the job—and Bryan was satisfied.

Colonel House, adroit, experienced in the ways of the world, was following one of the important rules of human relations: Always make the other person happy about doing the thing you suggest.

Woodrow Wilson followed that policy even when inviting William Gibbs McAdoo to become a member of his cabinet. That was the highest honor he could confer upon anyone, and yet Wilson extended the invitation in such a way as to make McAdoo feel doubly important. Here is the story in McAdoo's own words:

"He [Wilson] said that he was making up his cabinet and that he would be very glad if I would accept a place in it as Secretary of the Treasury. He had a delightful way of putting things; he created the impression that by accepting this great honor I would be doing him a favor."

Unfortunately, Wilson didn't always employ such tact. If he had, history might have been different. For example, Wilson didn't make the Senate and the Republican Party happy by entering the United States in the League of Nations. Wilson refused to take such prominent Republican leaders as Elihu Root or Charles Evans Hughes or Henry Cabot Lodge to the peace conference with him. Instead, he took along unknown men from his own party. He snubbed the Republicans, refused to let them feel that the League was their idea as well as his, refused to let them have a finger in the pie; and, as a result of this crude handling of human relations, wrecked his own career, ruined his health, shortened his life, caused America to stay out of the League, and altered the history of the world.

Statesmen and diplomats aren't the only ones who use this make-a-person-happy-to-do-things-you-want-them-to-do approach. Dale O. Ferrier of Fort Wayne, Indiana, told how he encouraged one of his young children to willingly do the chore he was assigned.

"One of Jeff's chores was to pick up pears from under the pear tree so the person who was mowing underneath wouldn't have to stop to pick them up. He didn't like this chore, and frequently it was either not done at all or it was done so poorly that the mower had to stop and pick up several pears that he had missed. Rather than have an eyeball-to-eyeball confrontation about it, one day I said to him, 'Jeff, I'll make a deal with you. For every bushel basket full of pears you pick up, I'll pay you one dollar. But after you are finished, for every pear I find left in the yard, I'll take away a dollar. How does that sound?' As you would expect, he not only picked up all of the pears, but I had to keep an eye on him to see that he didn't pull a few off the trees to fill up some of the baskets."

I knew a man who had to refuse many invitations to speak, invitations extended by friends, invitations coming from people to whom he was obligated; and yet he did it so adroitly that the other person was at least contented with his refusal. How did he do it? Not by merely talking about the fact that he was too busy and too-this and too-that. No, after expressing his appreciation of the invitation and regretting his inability to accept it, he suggested a substitute speaker. In other words, he didn't give the other person any time to feel unhappy about the refusal. He immediately changed the other person's thoughts to some other speaker who could accept the invitation.

Gunter Schmidt, who took our course in West Germany, told of an employee in the food store he managed who was negligent about putting the proper price tags on the shelves where the items were displayed. This caused confusion and customer complaints. Reminders, admonitions, confrontations with her about this did not do much good. Finally, Mr. Schmidt called her into his office and told her he was appointing her Supervisor of Price Tag Posting for the entire store and she would be responsible for keeping all of the shelves properly tagged. This new responsibility and title changed her attitude completely, and she fulfilled her duties satisfactorily from then on.

Childish? Perhaps. But that is what they said to Napoleon when he created the Legion of Honor and distributed 15,000 crosses to his soldiers and made eighteen of his generals "Marshals of France" and called his troops the "Grand Army." Napoleon was criticized for giving "toys" to war-hardened veterans, and Napoleon replied, "Men are ruled by toys."

This technique of giving titles and authority worked for Napoleon and it will work for you. For example, a friend of mine, Mrs. Ernest Gent of Scarsdale, New York, was troubled by boys running across and destroying her lawn. She tried criticism. She tried coaxing. Neither worked. Then she tried giving the worst sinner in the gang a title and a feeling of authority. She made him her "detective" and put him in charge of keeping all trespassers off her lawn. That solved her problem. Her "detective" built a bonfire in the backyard, heated an iron red-hot, and threatened to brand any boy who stepped on the lawn.

The effective leader should keep the following guidelines in mind when it is necessary to change attitudes or behavior:

1. Be sincere. Do not promise anything that you cannot deliver. Forget about the benefits to yourself and concentrate on the benefits to the other person.
2. Know exactly what it is you want the other person to do.
3. Be empathetic. Ask yourself what is it the other person really wants.
4. Consider the benefits that person will receive from doing what you suggest.
5. Match those benefits to the other person's wants.
6. When you make your request, put it in a form that will convey to the other person the idea that he personally will benefit. We could give a curt order like this: "John, we have customers coming in tomorrow and I need the stockroom cleaned out. So sweep it out, put the stock in neat piles on the shelves and polish the counter." Or we could express the same idea by showing John the benefits he will get from doing the task: "John, we have a job that should be completed right away. If it is done now, we won't be faced with it later. I am bringing some customers tomorrow to show our facilities. I would like to show them the stockroom, but it is in poor shape. If you could sweep it out, put the stock in neat piles on the shelves, and polish the counter, it would make us look efficient and you would have done your part to provide a good company image."

Will John be happy about doing what you suggest? Probably not very happy, but happier than if you had not pointed out the benefits. Assuming you know that John has pride in the way his stockroom looks and is interested in contributing to the company image, he will be more likely to be cooperative. It also will have been pointed out to John that the job would have to be done eventually and by doing it now, he won't be faced with it later.

It is naive to believe you will always get a favorable reaction from other persons when you use these approaches, but the experience of most people shows that you are more likely to change attitudes this way than by not using these principles—and if you increase your successes by even a mere 10 percent, you have become 10 percent more effective as a leader than you were before—and that is your benefit.

People are more likely to do what you would like them to do when you use...

⇒ PRINCIPLE 9 ⇐

Make the other person happy about doing the thing you suggest.

In a Nutshell

BE A LEADER

A leader's job often includes changing your people's attitudes and behavior. Some suggestions to accomplish this:

⇒ PRINCIPLE 1 ⇐

Begin with praise and honest appreciation.

⇒ PRINCIPLE 2 ⇐

Call attention to people's mistakes indirectly.

⇒ PRINCIPLE 3 ⇐

Talk about your own mistakes before criticizing the other person.

⇒ PRINCIPLE 4 ⇐

Ask questions instead of giving direct orders.

⇒ PRINCIPLE 5 ⇐

Let the other person save face.

⇒ PRINCIPLE 6 ⇐

Praise the slightest improvement and praise every improvement. Be "hearty in your approbation and lavish in your praise."

⇒ PRINCIPLE 7 ⇐

Give the other person a fine reputation to live up to.

⇒ PRINCIPLE 8 ⇐

Use encouragement. Make the fault seem easy to correct.

⇒ PRINCIPLE 9 ⇐

Make the other person happy about doing the thing you suggest.

"A Shortcut To Distinction"

by Lowell Thomas

This biographical information about Dale Carnegie was written as an introduction to the original edition of *How to Win Friends and Influence People*. It is reprinted in this edition to give the readers additional background on Dale Carnegie.

It was a cold January night in 1935, but the weather couldn't keep them away. Two thousand five hundred men and women thronged into the grand ballroom of the Hotel Pennsylvania in New York. Every available seat was filled by half-past seven. At eight o'clock, the eager crowd was still pouring in. The spacious balcony was soon jammed. Presently even standing space was at a premium, and hundreds of people, tired after navigating a day in business, stood up for an hour and a half that night to witness—what?

A fashion show?

A six-day bicycle race or a personal appearance by Clark Gable?

No. These people had been lured there by a newspaper ad. Two evenings previously, they had seen this full-page announcement in the *New York Sun* staring them in the face:

Learn to Speak Effectively Prepare for Leadership

Old stuff? Yes, but believe it or not, in the most sophisticated town on earth, during a depression with 20 percent of the population on relief, twenty-five hundred people had left their homes and hustled to the hotel in response to that ad.

The people who responded were of the upper economic strata—executives, employers and professionals.

These men and women had come to hear the opening gun of an ultramodern, ultrapractical course in "Effective Speaking and Influencing Men in Business"—a course given by the Dale Carnegie Institute of Effective Speaking and Human Relations.

Why were they there, these twenty-five hundred business men and women?

Because of a sudden hunger for more education because of the depression?

Apparently not, for this same course had been playing to packed houses in New York City every season for the preceding twenty-four years. During that time, more than fifteen thousand business and professional people had been trained by Dale Carnegie. Even large, skeptical, conservative organizations such as the Westinghouse Electric Company, the McGraw-Hill Publishing Company, the Brooklyn Union Gas Company, the Brooklyn Chamber of Commerce, the American Institute of Electrical Engineers and the New York Telephone Company have had this training conducted in their own offices for the benefit of their members and executives.

The fact that these people, ten or twenty years after leaving grade school, high school or college, come and take this training is a glaring commentary on the shocking deficiencies of our educational system.

What do adults really want to study? That is an important question; and in order to answer it, the University of Chicago, the American Association for Adult Education, and the United Y.M.C.A. Schools made a survey over a two-year period.

That survey revealed that the prime interest of adults is health. It also revealed that their second interest is in developing skill in human relationships—they want to learn the technique of getting along with and influencing other people. They don't want to become public speakers, and they don't want to listen to a lot of high-sounding talk about psychology; they want suggestions they can use immediately in business, in social contacts and in the home.

So that was what adults wanted to study, was it?

"All right," said the people making the survey. "Fine. If that is what they want, we'll give it to them."

Looking around for a textbook, they discovered that no working manual had ever been written to help people solve their daily problems in human relationships.

Here was a fine kettle of fish! For hundreds of years, learned volumes had been written on Greek and Latin and higher mathematics—topics about which the average adult doesn't give two hoots. But on the one subject on which he has a thirst for knowledge, a veritable passion for guidance and help—nothing!

This explained the presence of twenty-five hundred eager adults crowding into the grand ballroom of the Hotel Pennsylvania in response to a newspaper advertisement. Here, apparently, at last was the thing for which they had long been seeking.

Back in high school and college, they had pored over books, believing that knowledge alone was the open sesame to financial—and professional rewards.

But a few years in the rough-and-tumble of business and professional life had brought sharp disillusionment. They had seen some of the most important business successes won by men who possessed, in addition to their knowledge, the ability to talk well, to win people to their way of thinking, and to "sell" themselves and their ideas.

They soon discovered that if one aspired to wear the captain's cap and navigate the ship of business, personality and the ability to talk are more important than a knowledge of Latin verbs or a sheepskin from Harvard.

The advertisement in the *New York Sun* promised that the meeting would be highly entertaining. It was. Eighteen people who had taken the course were marshaled in front of the loudspeaker—and fifteen of them were given precisely seventy-five seconds each to tell his or her story. Only seventy-five seconds of talk, then "bang" went the gavel, and the chairman shouted, "Time! Next speaker!"

The affair moved with the speed of a herd of buffalo thundering across the plains. Spectators stood for an hour and a half to watch the performance.

The speakers were a cross section of life: several sales representatives, a chain-store executive, a baker, the president of a trade association, two bankers, an insurance agent, an accountant, a dentist, an architect, a druggist who had come from Indianapolis to New York to take the course, a lawyer who had come from Havana in order to prepare himself to give one important three-minute speech.

The first speaker bore the Gaelic name Patrick J. O'Haire. Born in Ireland, he attended school for only four years, drifted to America, worked as a mechanic, then as a chauffeur.

Now, however, he was forty, he had a growing family and needed more money, so he tried selling trucks. Suffering from an inferiority complex that, as he put it, was eating his heart out, he had to walk up and down in front of an office half a dozen times before he could summon up enough courage to open the door. He was so discouraged as a salesman that he was thinking of going back to working with his hands in a machine shop, when one day he received a letter inviting him to an organization meeting of the Dale Carnegie Course in Effective Speaking.

He didn't want to attend. He feared he would have to associate with a lot of college graduates, that he would be out of place.

His despairing wife insisted that he go, saying, "It may do you some good, Pat. God knows you need it." He went down to the place where the meeting was to be held and stood on the sidewalk for five minutes before he could generate enough self-confidence to enter the room.

The first few times he tried to speak in front of the others, he was dizzy with fear. But as the weeks drifted by, he lost all fear of audiences and soon found that he loved to talk—the bigger the crowd, the better. And he also lost his fear of individuals and of his superiors. He presented his ideas to them, and soon he advanced into the sales department. He had become a valued and much liked member of his company. That night, in the Hotel Pennsylvania, Patrick O'Haire stood in front of twenty-five hundred people and told a gay, rollicking story of his achievements. Wave after wave of laughter swept over the audience. Few professional speakers could have equaled his performance.

The next speaker, Godfrey Meyer, was a gray-headed banker, the father of eleven children. The first time he had attempted to speak in class, he was literally struck dumb. His story is a vivid illustration of how leadership gravitates to the person who can talk.

He worked on Wall Street, and for twenty-five years he had been living in Clifton, New Jersey. During that time, he had taken no active part in community affairs and knew perhaps five hundred people.

Shortly after he had enrolled in the Carnegie course, he received his tax bill and was infuriated by what he considered unjust charges. Ordinarily, he would have sat at home and fumed, or he would have taken it out in grousing to his neighbors. But instead, he put on his hat that night, walked into the town meeting, and blew off steam in public.

As a result of that talk of indignation, the citizens of Clifton, New Jersey, urged him to run for the town council. So for weeks he went from one meeting to another, denouncing waste and municipal extravagance.

There were ninety-six candidates in the field. When the ballots were counted, lo, Godfrey Meyer's name led all the rest. Almost overnight, he had become a public figure among the forty thousand people in his community. As a result of his talks, he made eighty times more friends in six weeks than he had been able to previously in twenty-five years.

And his salary as councilman meant that he got a return of 1,000 percent a year on his investment in the Carnegie course.

The third speaker, the head of a large national association of food manufacturers, told how he had been unable to stand up and express his ideas at meetings of a board of directors.

As a result of learning to think on his feet, two astonishing things happened. He was soon made president of his association, and in that capacity, he was obliged to address meetings all over the United States. Excerpts from his talks were put on the Associated Press wires and printed in newspapers and trade magazines throughout the country.

In two years, after learning to speak more effectively, he received more free publicity for his company and its products than he had been able to get previously with a quarter of a million dollars spent in direct advertising. This speaker admitted that he had formerly hesitated to telephone some of the more important business executives in Manhattan and invite them to lunch with him. But as a result of the prestige he had acquired by his talks, these same people telephoned him and invited him to lunch and apologized to him for encroaching on his time.

The ability to speak is a shortcut to distinction. It puts a person in the limelight, raises one head and shoulders above the crowd. And the person who can speak acceptably is usually given credit for an ability out of all proportion to what he or she really possesses.

A movement for adult education has been sweeping over the nation; and the most spectacular force in that movement was Dale Carnegie, a man who listened to and critiqued more talks by adults than has any other man in captivity. According to a cartoon by "Believe-It-or-Not" Ripley, he had criticized 150,000 speeches. If that grand total doesn't impress you, remember that it meant one talk for almost every day that has passed since Columbus discovered America. Or, to put it in other words, if all the people who had spoken before him had used only three minutes and had appeared before him in succession, it would have taken ten months, listening day and night, to hear them all.

Dale Carnegie's own career, filled with sharp contrasts, was a striking example of what a person can accomplish when obsessed with an original idea and afire with enthusiasm.

Born on a Missouri farm ten miles from a railway, he never saw a streetcar until he was twelve years old; yet by the time he was forty-six, he was familiar with the far-flung corners of the earth, everywhere from Hong Kong to Hammerfest; and, at one time, he approached closer to the North Pole than Admiral Byrd's headquarters at Little America was to the South Pole.

This Missouri lad who had once picked strawberries and cut cockleburs for five cents an hour became the highly paid trainer of the executives of large corporations in the art of self-expression.

This erstwhile cowboy who had once punched cattle and branded calves and ridden fences out in western South Dakota later went to London to put on shows under the patronage of the royal family.

This chap who was a total failure the first half-dozen times he tried to speak in public later became my personal manager. Much of my success has been due to training under Dale Carnegie.

Young Carnegie had to struggle for an education, for hard luck was always battering away at the old farm in northwest Missouri with a flying tackle and a body slam. Year after year, the "102" River rose and drowned the corn and swept away the hay. Season after season, the fat hogs sickened and died from cholera, the bottom fell out of the market for cattle and mules, and the bank threatened to foreclose the mortgage.

Sick with discouragement, the family sold out and bought another farm near the State Teachers' College at Warrensburg, Missouri. Board and room could be had in town for a dollar a day, but young Carnegie couldn't afford it. So he stayed on the farm and commuted on horseback three miles to college each day. At home, he milked the cows, cut the wood, fed the hogs, and studied his Latin verbs by the light of a coal-oil lamp until his eyes blurred and he began to nod.

Even when he got to bed at midnight, he set the alarm for three o'clock. His father bred pedigreed Duroc-Jersey hogs—and there was danger, during the bitter cold nights, that the young pigs would freeze to death; so they were put in a basket, covered with a gunny sack, and set behind the kitchen stove. True to their nature, the pigs demanded a hot meal at 3 A.M. So when the alarm went off, Dale Carnegie crawled out of the blankets, took the basket of pigs out to their mother, waited for them to nurse, and then brought them back to the warmth of the kitchen stove.

There were six hundred students in State Teachers' College, and Dale Carnegie was one of the isolated half-dozen who couldn't afford to board in town. He was ashamed of the poverty that made it necessary for him to ride back to the farm and milk the cows every night. He was ashamed of his coat, which was too tight, and his trousers, which were too short.

Rapidly developing an inferiority complex, he looked about for some shortcut to distinction. He soon saw that there were certain groups in college that enjoyed influence and prestige—the football and baseball players and the chaps who won the debating and public-speaking contests.

Realizing that he had no flair for athletics, he decided to win one of the speaking contests. He spent months preparing his talks. He practiced as he sat in the saddle galloping to college and back; he practiced his speeches as he milked the cows; and then he mounted a bale of hay in the barn and with great gusto and gestures harangued the frightened pigeons about the issues of the day.

But in spite of all his earnestness and preparation, he met with defeat after defeat. He was eighteen at the time—sensitive and proud. He became so discouraged, so depressed, that he even thought of suicide. And then suddenly he began to win, not one contest, but every speaking contest in college.

Other students pleaded with him to train them; and they won also.

After graduating from college, he started selling correspondence courses to the ranchers among the sand hills of western Nebraska and eastern Wyoming. In spite of all his boundless energy and enthusiasm, he couldn't make the grade. He became so discouraged that he went to his hotel room in Alliance, Nebraska, in the middle of the day, threw himself across the bed, and wept in despair. He longed to go back to college, he longed to retreat from the harsh battle of life; but he couldn't. So he resolved to go to Omaha and get another job. He didn't have the money for a railroad ticket, so he traveled on a freight train, feeding and watering two carloads of wild horses in return for his passage. After landing in south Omaha, he got a job selling bacon and soap and lard for Armour and Company. His territory was up among the Badlands and the cow and Indian country of western South Dakota. He covered his territory by freight train and stagecoach and horseback and slept in pioneer hotels where the only partition between the rooms was a sheet of muslin. He studied books on salesmanship, rode bucking broncos, played poker with the Indians, and learned how to collect money. And when, for example, an inland storekeeper couldn't pay cash for the bacon and hams he had ordered, Dale Carnegie would take a dozen pairs of shoes off his shelf, sell the shoes to the railroad men, and forward the receipts to Armour and Company.

He would often ride a freight train a hundred miles a day. When the train stopped to unload freight, he would dash uptown, see three or four merchants, get his orders; and when the whistle blew, he would dash down the street again lickety-split and swing onto the train while it was moving.

Within two years, he had taken an unproductive territory that had stood in the twenty-fifth place and had boosted it to first place among all the twenty-nine car routes leading out of south Omaha. Armour and Company offered to promote him, saying: "You have achieved what seemed impossible." But he refused the promotion and resigned, went to New York, studied at the American Academy of Dramatic Arts, and toured the country, playing the role of Dr. Hartley in *Polly of the Circus*.

He would never be a Booth or a Barrymore. He had the good sense to recognize that. So back he went to sales work, selling automobiles and trucks for the Packard Motor Car Company.

He knew nothing about machinery and cared nothing about it. Dreadfully unhappy, he had to scourge himself to his task each day. He longed to have time to study, to write the books he had dreamed about writing back in college. So he resigned. He was going to spend his days writing stories and novels and support himself by teaching in a night school.

Teaching what? As he looked back and evaluated his college work, he saw that his training in public speaking had done more to give him confidence, courage, poise and the ability to meet and deal with people in business than had all the rest of his college courses put together, so he urged the Y.M.C.A. schools in New York to give him a chance to conduct courses in public speaking for people in business.

What? Make orators out of business people? Absurd. The Y.M.C.A. people knew. They had tried such courses—and they had always failed. When they refused to pay him a salary of two dollars a night, he agreed to teach on a commission basis and take a percentage of the net profits—if there were any profits to take. And inside of three years they were paying him thirty dollars a night on that basis—instead of two.

The course grew. Other 'Ys' heard of it, then other cities. Dale Carnegie soon became a glorified circuit rider covering New York, Philadelphia, Baltimore and later London and Paris. All the textbooks were too academic and impractical for the business people who flocked to his courses. Because of this he wrote his own book entitled *Public Speaking and Influencing Men in Business*. It became the official text of all the Y.M.C.A.s as well as of the American Bankers' Association and the National Credit Men's Association.

Dale Carnegie claimed that all people can talk when they get mad. He said that if you hit the most ignorant man in town on the jaw and knock him down, he would get on his feet and talk with an eloquence, heat and emphasis that would have rivaled that world-famous orator William Jennings Bryan at the height of his career. He claimed that almost any person can speak acceptably in public if he or she has self-confidence and an idea that is boiling and stewing within.

The way to develop self-confidence, he said, is to do the thing you fear to do and get a record of successful experiences behind you. So he forced each class member to talk at every session of the course. The audience is sympathetic. They are all in the same boat; and, by constant practice, they develop a courage, confidence and enthusiasm that carry over into their private speaking.

Dale Carnegie would tell you that he made a living all these years, not by teaching public speaking - that was incidental. His main job was to help people conquer their fears and develop courage.

He started out at first to conduct merely a course in public speaking, but the students who came were businessmen and women. Many of them hadn't seen the inside of a classroom in thirty years. Most of them were paying their tuition on the installment plan. They wanted results and they wanted them quick—results that they could use the next day in business interviews and in speaking before groups.

So he was forced to be swift and practical. Consequently, he developed a system of training that is unique—a striking combination of public speaking, salesmanship, human relations and applied psychology.

A slave to no hard-and-fast rules, he developed a course that is as real as the measles and twice as much fun.

When the classes terminated, the graduates formed clubs of their own and continued to meet fortnightly for years afterward. One group of nineteen in Philadelphia met twice a month during the winter season for seventeen years. Class members frequently travel fifty or a hundred miles to attend classes. One student used to commute each week from Chicago to New York. Professor William James of Harvard used to say that the average person develops only 10 percent of his latent mental ability. Dale Carnegie, by helping businessmen and women to develop their latent possibilities, created one of the most significant movements in adult education.

– Lowell Thomas

1936